FAST
seafood

THE AUSTRALIAN
Women's Weekly

FAST
seafood

acp
books

contents

Clean, fresh seafood is a naturally occuring "fast food". Easy and quick to prepare, it's at its best when cooked briefly and pretty much left alone, served with a sauce, strewn or stuffed with fresh herbs, or plunged at the last minute into a luscious broth that's ready and waiting. Overcooked seafood tends to be dry and unappetising so it's best removed from the stove when just a tad underdone since the residual heat will continue to cook it slightly. Fresh seafood will have virtually no odour; the eyes will be clear and bulge a little, and the flesh will be firm, shiny and spring back when pressed. Rinse fresh fish under cold running water, pat dry with absorbent paper then keep it loosely wrapped but air-tight in the coldest part of your refrigerator for no more than two days after purchase. Seafood is an excellent source of lean, easily digestible protein and many minerals, while being low in fat, cholesterol and sodium. In general, seafood is one of the most well-balanced foods, and a diet containing a variety of seafood helps maintain a healthy nutrient intake compatible with a low-fat diet.

finger food+
starters

Crab dip

200g packaged cream cheese
¼ cup (75g) mayonnaise
2 tablespoons lime juice
1 tablespoon sweet chilli sauce
1 dill pickle (50g), chopped finely
2 x 170g cans crab meat, drained, flaked
2 tablespoons finely chopped fresh coriander

1 Beat cheese, mayonnaise, juice and sauce in small bowl with electric mixer until smooth. Transfer to serving bowl; fold in remaining ingredients.
2 Serve cold with toasted french bread slices.

on the table in 15 minutes
makes 2 cups **per tablespoon** 3.8g total fat (1.9g saturated fat); 205kJ (49 cal); 1.6g carbohydrate; 2g protein; 0.1g fibre
tip dip can be made up to 4 hours ahead. Cover; refrigerate until required.

Oysters with chilli-lime dressing

24 oysters, on the half shell
½ teaspoon finely grated lime rind
¼ cup (60ml) lime juice
2 teaspoons white sugar
1 kaffir lime leaf, shredded finely
2 fresh small red thai chillies, sliced thinly
2 tablespoons peanut oil

1 Carefully remove oysters from shells; wash and dry shells. Return oysters to shells; place, in single layer, on serving platter.
2 Place remaining ingredients in screw-top jar; shake well. Drizzle dressing among oysters.

on the table in 10 minutes
makes 24 **per oyster** 2.1g total fat (0.5g saturated fat); 138kJ (33 cal); 0.6g carbohydrate; 3g protein; 0g fibre
tip dressing can be made a day ahead.

Fresh prawn spring rolls

125g rice vermicelli noodles
2 tablespoons lime juice
2 tablespoons palm sugar
1 tablespoon fish sauce
1 lebanese cucumber (130g), seeded
16 x 16cm-round rice paper sheets
16 large fresh mint leaves
16 cooked medium prawns (560g), shelled, deveined
6 green onions, sliced thinly
16 sprigs fresh coriander
1 cup (50g) snow pea sprouts
dipping sauce
½ cup (125ml) sweet chilli sauce
2 tablespoons lime juice

1 Make dipping sauce.
2 Place noodles in medium bowl of hot water about 5 minutes or until softened; drain well. Chop noodles coarsely.
3 Combine noodles with juice, sugar and fish sauce in medium bowl. Cut cucumber into thin strips.
4 Place 1 sheet of rice paper in medium bowl of warm water until just softened; lift from water carefully, place on board covered with tea towel. Top with mint, prawn and 1 heaped tablespoon of the noodle mixture, cucumber, green onions, coriander and sprouts. Fold in two opposing sides; roll to enclose filling. Repeat with remaining rice paper sheets and remaining ingredients. Place rolls on tray lined with plastic wrap; cover with damp paper towel and refrigerate until ready to serve.
dipping sauce combine sauce and juice in small bowl.

on the table in 30 minutes
serves 4 **per serving** 2.5g total fat (0.4g saturated fat); 1396kJ (334 cal); 49.9g carbohydrate; 25g protein; 4g fibre

Oysters with mango and chilli

12 oysters, on the half shell
½ firm small mango (150g), chopped finely
1 fresh small red thai chilli, chopped finely
1 teaspoon lime juice

1 Carefully remove oysters from shells; wash and dry shells. Return oysters to shells; place, in single layer, on serving platter.
2 Combine remaining ingredients in small bowl; divide mango mixture among oysters.

on the table in 10 minutes
makes 12 **per oyster** 0.3g total fat (0.1g saturated fat); 54kJ (13 cal); 1.2g carbohydrate; 1.3g protein; 0.1g fibre
tip mango mixture can be made a day ahead. Cover; refrigerate until required.

Salmon and herb soufflés

415g can red salmon, drained, flaked
2 tablespoons chopped fresh chives
2 tablespoons chopped fresh flat-leaf parsley
pinch cayenne pepper
40g butter
2 tablespoons plain flour
1 cup (250ml) milk
4 egg whites

1 Preheat oven to 180°C/160°C fan-forced. Oil four soufflé
(1-cup/250ml) dishes.
2 Combine salmon, herbs and pepper in large bowl; mix well.
3 Heat butter in small saucepan, stir in flour; cook until bubbling,
remove from heat. Gradually stir in milk; stir over heat until sauce
boils and thickens. Stir sauce into salmon mixture.
4 Beat egg whites with electric mixer until soft peaks form; fold into
salmon mixture. Spoon mixture into dishes.
5 Bake 20 minutes or until risen and well browned; serve immediately.

on the table in 35 minutes
serves 4 **per serving** 20.8g total fat (9.8g saturated fat); 1317kJ
(315 cal); 7.3g carbohydrate; 24.8g protein; 0.4g fibre

Calamari rings with chermoulla

1kg calamari rings
1½ teaspoons chilli powder
3 teaspoons garlic salt
½ cup (75g) plain flour
vegetable oil, for shallow-frying
chermoulla
½ teaspoon hot paprika
1 fresh small red thai chilli, chopped finely
1 small red onion (100g), chopped finely
1 tablespoon finely grated lemon rind
2 cloves garlic, crushed
¼ cup (60ml) lemon juice
⅓ cup (80ml) olive oil
½ cup chopped fresh flat-leaf parsley

1 Make chermoulla.
2 Toss calamari in combined chilli powder, salt and flour in medium bowl; shake away excess flour mixture.
3 Heat oil in large frying pan; cook calamari, in batches, until browned and tender, drain on absorbent paper.
4 Serve calamari with chermoulla.
chermoulla combine ingredients in small bowl.

on the table in 20 minutes
serves 4 **per serving** 34.2g total fat (5.2g saturated fat); 2295kJ (549 cal); 15.5g carbohydrate; 44.5g protein; 1.8g fibre

Oysters with tomato-capsicum salsa

24 oysters, on the half shell
2 small vine-ripened tomatoes (180g), seeded, chopped finely
1 small red onion (100g), chopped finely
1 small green capsicum (150g), chopped finely
¼ cup (60ml) tomato juice
¼ cup (60ml) lemon juice
1 teaspoon Tabasco sauce
1 tablespoon olive oil
2 cloves garlic, crushed

1 Carefully remove oysters from shells; wash and dry shells. Return oysters to shells; place, in single layer, on serving platter.
2 Combine remaining ingredients in small bowl; divide salsa among oysters.

on the table in 10 minutes
makes 24 **per oyster** 1.4g total fat (0.3g saturated fat); 121kJ (29 cal); 0.9g carbohydrate; 3.2g protein; 0.3g fibre
tip salsa can be made a day ahead. Cover; refrigerate until required.

Chilli scallops

1 tablespoon peanut oil
32 small scallops
4 cloves garlic, sliced thinly
5cm piece fresh ginger (25g), sliced thinly
2 fresh small red thai chillies, chopped finely
3 green onions, sliced thinly
⅓ cup (80ml) sweet chilli sauce
1 teaspoon fish sauce
2 teaspoons brown sugar
½ cup (125ml) chicken stock
¼ cup coarsely chopped fresh coriander

1 Heat half of the oil in wok; stir-fry scallops, in batches, until just changed in colour.
2 Heat remaining oil in wok; stir fry garlic, ginger, chilli and onion until onion is soft. Stir in combined sauces, sugar and stock; bring to a boil.
3 Return scallops to wok; stir until heated through. Serve scallops sprinkled with coriander.

on the table in 30 minutes
serves 4 **per serving** 6.8g total fat (1.4g saturated fat); 811kJ (194 cal); 8.1g carbohydrate; 24.3g protein; 1.9g fibre
tips we used scallops with roe in this recipe; but the roe can be left out if you prefer. If you buy scallops in their shell, don't discard the shell, they are great (washed and dried) to use as serving "dishes".

Mussels with avocado and pickled ginger

12 large black mussels (600g)
½ cup (125ml) water
½ firm medium avocado (125g), chopped finely
1 tablespoon drained pickled ginger, chopped finely
1 shallot (25g), chopped finely
1 tablespoon lime juice

1 Scrub mussels; remove beards.
2 Bring the water to a boil in medium saucepan; cook mussels, covered, about 5 minutes or until mussels open (discard any that do not). Drain; discard liquid. Break open shells; discard tops. Loosen mussels from bottom shells with a spoon; place mussels in shells, in single layer, on serving platter. Cover; refrigerate 15 minutes or until cold.
3 Combine remaining ingredients in small bowl; divide avocado mixture among mussels.

on the table in 35 minutes
makes 12 **per mussel** 1.9g total fat (0.4g saturated fat); 105kJ (25 cal); 0.6g carbohydrate; 1.4g protein; 0.2g fibre
tip use a stiff brush to scrub the mussels under cold water.

Chilli salt squid

1kg whole small squid
vegetable or peanut oil, for deep-frying
2 fresh medium red chillies, sliced thinly
1 cup loosely packed fresh coriander leaves
⅓ cup (50g) plain flour
2 fresh medium red chillies, chopped finely, extra
2 teaspoons sea salt
1 teaspoon ground black pepper

1 Clean squid by gently pulling head and tentacles away from body. Remove clear backbone (quill) from inside body. Cut tentacles from head just below eyes; discard head. Remove side fins and skin from body with salted fingers. Rinse body, tentacles and fins if necessary.
2 Cut body to open out flat. Using a sharp knife, lightly score inside flesh in a diagonal pattern. Cut tentacles into pieces and fins into strips. Pat squid dry with absorbent paper.
3 Carefully (the oil will spit) deep-fry chilli in hot oil until softened; drain on absorbent paper. Deep-fry coriander carefully (oil will spit) for 10 seconds or until changed in colour; drain on absorbent paper.
4 Toss squid in combined flour, extra chilli, salt and pepper. Shake away excess. Deep-fry squid, in batches, until just browned and tender; drain on absorbent paper. Sprinkle squid with deep-fried coriander and chilli.

on the table in 30 minutes
serves 8 **per serving** 3.7g total fat (0.6g saturated fat); 389kJ (93 cal); 4.8g carbohydrate; 9.9g protein; 0.5g fibre
tip squid is best eaten as soon as it is cooked, but can be kept warm, on an absorbent-paper-lined tray, in a very slow oven while cooking in batches.

Mini prawn laksa

You need 24 shot glasses for this recipe.

600g cooked small prawns
2 teaspoons peanut oil
¼ cup (75g) laksa paste
1 clove garlic, crushed
1 fresh kaffir lime leaf, sliced thinly
½ teaspoon ground turmeric
1 green onion, sliced thinly
140ml can coconut milk
1½ cups (375ml) water
2 tablespoons lime juice
3 teaspoons fish sauce
24 fresh small coriander leaves

1 Shell and devein prawns, leaving tails intact; reserve prawn heads.
2 Heat oil in medium saucepan; cook paste, garlic, lime leaf, turmeric, onion and prawn heads, stirring, until fragrant. Add coconut milk and the water; bring to a boil. Reduce heat, simmer, covered, 10 minutes.
3 Strain laksa through sieve into large jug; discard solids. Stir juice and sauce into laksa.
4 Divide laksa among glasses, place 1 prawn over rim of each glass; top each with coriander leaf. Serve warm.

on the table in 25 minutes
makes 24 **per shot** 1.7g total fat (1.1g saturated fat); 130kJ (31 cal); 0.3g carbohydrate; 2.8g protein; 0.2g fibre

Oysters with green olive paste

24 oysters, on the half shell
½ cup (60g) seeded green olives
2 teaspoons olive oil
¼ cup (60ml) red wine vinegar
2 cloves garlic, quartered
2 tablespoons toasted pine nuts
2 teaspoons coarsely chopped fresh lemon thyme

1 Carefully remove oysters from shells; wash and dry shells. Return
oysters to shells; place, in single layer, on serving platter.
2 Blend or process olives, oil, vinegar, garlic and pine nuts until mixture
forms a paste. Top oysters with paste; sprinkle with thyme.

on the table in 10 minutes
makes 24 **per oyster** 1.9g total fat (0.3g saturated fat); 131kJ (31.4 cal);
0.4g carbohydrate; 3.2g protein; 0.2g fibre

Salt and pepper baby octopus with aïoli

500g cleaned baby octopus, halved lengthways
2 teaspoons sea salt
3 teaspoons cracked black pepper
150g mesclun
1 lebanese cucumber (130g), sliced thinly
125g cherry tomatoes, halved
2 tablespoons olive oil
dressing
1 tablespoon lemon juice
1 tablespoon olive oil
aïoli
1 egg yolk
1 clove garlic, crushed
1 teaspoon dijon mustard
1 tablespoon white wine vinegar
1 cup (250ml) olive oil
1 teaspoon lemon juice

1 Make dressing and aïoli.
2 Combine octopus, salt and pepper in medium bowl.
3 Place mesclun, cucumber, tomato and dressing in large bowl; toss gently to combine.
4 Heat oil in wok; stir-fry octopus, in batches, until browned lightly and cooked through.
5 Serve octopus on salad with aïoli and lemon wedges, if desired.
dressing place ingredients in screw-top jar; shake well.
aïoli blend or process egg yolk, garlic, mustard and vinegar until combined. With motor operating, gradually add oil in thin, steady stream; process until aïoli thickens slightly. Stir in juice.

on the table in 20 minutes
serves 4 **per serving** 74.3g total fat (10.9g saturated fat); 3348kJ (801 cal); 3.5g carbohydrate; 31.4g protein; 2.1g fibre
tips you can double or treble this aïoli recipe, if you like, but don't throw the egg whites away. Freeze them until you have enough to make a pavlova or friands. If the aïoli you've made separates, place a yolk in another bowl and whisk the separated aïoli into it. The added yolk will re-emulsify the sauce.

Prawn remoulade

3 egg yolks
1 tablespoon white wine vinegar
1 tablespoon wholegrain mustard
¼ cup (60ml) water
1⅓ cups (330ml) vegetable oil
2 tablespoons drained capers, chopped finely
2 tablespoons fresh dill, chopped coarsely
48 cooked medium prawns (1.6kg)

1 Blend or process yolks, vinegar, mustard and the water until smooth.
With motor operating, gradually add oil in a thin, steady stream; process
until mixture thickens. Transfer mixture to medium serving bowl; stir in
capers and dill. Cover; refrigerate until cold.
2 Meanwhile, shell and devein prawns, leaving tails intact. Arrange
prawns on serving platter. Serve with remoulade.

on the table in 35 minutes
makes 48 prawns & 2 cups remoulade
per prawn 13.2g total fat (1.7g saturated fat); 627kJ (150 cal);
0.1g carbohydrate; 8.1g protein; 0g fibre
tip remoulade can be made up to a day ahead. Cover; refrigerate
until required.

Tuna carpaccio with lemon oil and baby capers

400g sashimi tuna, sliced thinly
1 tablespoon extra virgin olive oil
¼ cup (50g) drained baby capers
2 tablespoons finely shredded lemon rind
2 tablespoons extra virgin olive oil, extra
1 tablespoon chopped fresh flat-leaf parsley

1 Using a meat mallet, pound tuna between sheets of plastic wrap until paper-thin; arrange on serving plates.
2 Heat oil in small frying pan; cook capers, stirring, until crisp. Drain on absorbent paper.
3 Combine rind with extra oil in small jug; drizzle over tuna. Serve tuna sprinkled with capers and parsley.

on the table in 20 minutes
serves 6 **per serving** 12.9g total fat (2.8g saturated fat); 777kJ (186 cal); 0.8g carbohydrate; 16.8g protein; 0.3g fibre
tip tuna sold as sashimi tuna has met stringent guidelines regarding its treatment since leaving the water, so you can be guaranteed of its quality and that it's safe to eat raw.

Scallops with saffron cream

12 scallops in half shell (480g)
1 teaspoon olive oil
1 small brown onion (80g), chopped finely
2 teaspoons finely grated lemon rind
pinch saffron threads
⅔ cup (160ml) cream
1 tablespoon lemon juice
2 teaspoons salmon roe

1 Remove scallops from shells; wash and dry shells. Place shells, in single layer, on serving platter.
2 Rinse scallops under cold water; discard scallop roe. Gently pat scallops dry with absorbent paper.
3 Heat oil in small saucepan; cook onion, stirring, until softened. Add rind, saffron and cream; bring to a boil. Reduce heat, simmer, uncovered, about 5 minutes or until mixture has reduced to about ½ cup. Remove from heat; stand 20 minutes. Stir in juice. Strain cream mixture into small bowl then back into same cleaned pan; stir over low heat until heated through.
4 Meanwhile, cook scallops, in batches, on heated oiled grill plate (or grill or barbecue) until browned lightly and cooked as desired.
5 Return scallops to shells; top with cream sauce and roe.

on the table in 35 minutes
makes 12 **per scallop** 6.4g total fat (4g saturated fat); 288kJ (69 cal); 0.8g carbohydrate; 2.3g protein; 0.1g fibre

Smoked seafood and mixed vegetable antipasti

⅓ cup (80g) sour cream
2 teaspoons raspberry vinegar
1 tablespoon coarsely chopped fresh chives
1 clove garlic, crushed
1 large yellow zucchini (150g)
1 tablespoon raspberry vinegar, extra
¼ cup (60ml) extra virgin olive oil
⅓ cup (45g) toasted slivered almonds
1 cup (150g) drained semi-dried tomatoes
1 large avocado (320g)
1 tablespoon lemon juice
300g hot-smoked ocean trout portions
200g sliced smoked salmon
16 drained caperberries (80g)
1 lemon, cut into wedges
170g packet roasted garlic bagel crisps

1 Combine sour cream, vinegar, chives and garlic in small bowl.
Cover; refrigerate until required.
2 Meanwhile, using vegetable peeler, slice zucchini lengthways
into ribbons. Combine zucchini ribbons in small bowl with extra
vinegar and 2 tablespoons of the oil.
3 Combine nuts, tomatoes and remaining oil in small bowl. Slice
avocado thickly into small bowl; sprinkle with juice. Flake trout into
bite-sized pieces.
4 Arrange zucchini mixture, nut mixture, avocado, trout, salmon and
caperberries on large platter; serve with sour cream mixture, lemon
and bagel crisps.

on the table in 35 minutes
serves 4 **per serving** 54.8g total fat (12.7g saturated fat); 3189kJ
(763 cal); 20.2g carbohydrate; 44.5g protein; 8.8g fibre
tip hot-smoked trout is now available at most supermarkets in filleted
portions of various sizes; we used two 150g portions for this recipe.

Prawns with chilli, coriander and lime butter

16 uncooked large king prawns (1.1kg)
100g butter
2 fresh small red thai chillies, chopped finely
2 tablespoons lime juice
2 tablespoons finely chopped fresh coriander
50g mesclun

1 Shell and devein prawns, leaving tails intact; cut lengthways along prawn backs, without separating.
2 Melt butter in wok; stir-fry prawns, in batches, until changed in colour and just cooked through.
3 Return prawns to wok. Add chilli, juice and coriander; toss gently to combine. Divide prawns and mesclun among serving plates

on the table in 15 minutes
serves 4 **per serving** 21.4g total fat (13.6g saturated fat); 1287kJ (308 cal); 0.5g carbohydrate; 21.4g protein; 0.4g fibre
tip you can use scampi or yabbies as a substitute for the prawns, if you like.

Tarragon and lime scallops

You need 24 bamboo skewers for this recipe; soak them in cold water for at least an hour prior to use to prevent splintering or scorching.

24 scallops (600g), roe removed
2 tablespoons coarsely chopped fresh tarragon
1 tablespoon lime juice
1 tablespoon olive oil
3 limes

1 Rinse scallops under cold water; dry with absorbent paper. Combine scallops, tarragon, juice and oil in medium bowl.
2 Cut each lime into eight wedges. Thread one scallop and one lime wedge on each skewer. Cook, in batches, on heated oiled grill plate (or grill or barbecue) until scallops are cooked through. Serve hot.

on the table in 25 minutes
makes 24 **per skewer** 0.9g total fat (0.2g saturated fat); 92kJ (22 cal); 0.2g carbohydrate; 3g protein; 0.1g fibre
tip uncooked scallops and lime wedges can be skewered up to 4 hours ahead. Cover; refrigerate until required.

Tuna tartare on crunchy wonton triangles

100g sashimi tuna, chopped finely
½ small red onion (50g), chopped finely
1 tablespoon finely chopped fresh mint
1 tablespoon finely chopped fresh coriander
1 tablespoon lime juice
1 tablespoon fish sauce
6 square wonton wrappers
vegetable oil, for deep-frying
24 fresh baby coriander leaves

1 Combine tuna, onion, mint, coriander, juice and sauce in small bowl.
2 Cut each wrapper into four triangles. Heat oil in wok; deep-fry triangles, in batches, until crisp. Drain on absorbent paper.
3 Place triangles on serving platter; top with a heaped teaspoon of tuna mixture then 1 coriander leaf.

on the table in 30 minutes
makes 24 **per piece** 0.4g total fat (0.1g saturated fat); 59kJ (14 cal); 1.3g carbohydrate; 1.4g protein; 0.1g fibre
tip tuna sold as sashimi tuna has met stringent guidelines regarding its treatment since leaving the water, so you can be guaranteed of its quality and that it's safe to eat raw.

Salmon tartare

250g sashimi salmon, chopped finely
1 small red onion (100g), chopped finely
2 tablespoons lemon juice
2 teaspoons prepared horseradish
1 tablespoon drained capers, chopped finely
2 tablespoons finely chopped fresh chives
80g packet mini toasts
¼ cup (65g) crème fraîche
40 small fresh dill sprigs

1 Place salmon and onion in medium bowl with combined juice,
horseradish, capers and chives; toss gently to combine.
2 Divide salmon tartare among mini toasts; top each with crème fraîche
and a dill sprig. Serve cold.

on the table in 30 minutes
makes 40 **per toast** 0.4g total fat (0.1g saturated fat); 59kJ (14 cal);
1.3g carbohydrate; 1.4g protein; 0.1g fibre
tips salmon sold as sashimi salmon has met stringent guidelines
regarding its treatment since leaving the water, so you can be guaranteed
of its quality and that it's safe to eat raw. Tartare ingredients can be
chopped up to 3 hours ahead of combining. Cover separately; refrigerate
until required.

Tikka prawns with raita

24 uncooked large king prawns (1.6kg)
¼ cup (70g) tikka paste
1½ cups (420g) yogurt
¼ cup finely chopped fresh coriander
½ teaspoon ground cumin

1 Shell and devein prawns, leaving tails intact.
2 Combine paste and ½ cup of the yogurt in small bowl.
3 Cook prawns, in batches, on heated oiled grill plate (or grill or barbecue),
brushing prawns with paste mixture, until just changed in colour.
4 Meanwhile, combine remaining yogurt in small bowl with coriander
and cumin.
5 Serve prawns hot, with raita.

on the table in 30 minutes
makes 24 **per prawn** 1.7g total fat (0.5g saturated fat); 217kJ (52 cal);
1.1g carbohydrate; 7.8g protein; 0.3g fibre
tip uncooked prawns can be marinated and raita made a day ahead.
Cover separately; refrigerate until required.

Spicy crab and prawn fritters with chilli lime dipping sauce

650g uncooked large king prawns
2 x 170g cans crab meat, drained
1 tablespoon red curry paste
1 egg
2 green onions, chopped coarsely
2 tablespoons coarsely chopped fresh coriander
2 teaspoons coarsely chopped fresh lemon grass
1 fresh small red thai chilli, chopped coarsely
2 tablespoons peanut oil
chilli lime dipping sauce
2 tablespoons lime juice
2 tablespoons water
2 teaspoons fish sauce
2 teaspoons white sugar
1 kaffir lime leaf, shredded finely
1 fresh small red thai chilli, chopped finely

1 Shell and devein prawns; blend or process with crab, paste, egg, onion, coriander, lemon grass and chilli until just combined. Using hands, shape level tablespoons of mixture into fritter shapes.
2 Make chilli lime dipping sauce.
3 Heat oil in large frying pan; cook fritters, in batches, until golden brown and cooked through. Drain on absorbent paper.
4 Serve fritters with chilli lime dipping sauce.
chilli lime dipping sauce whisk ingredients together in small bowl until sugar dissolves.

on the table in 30 minutes
makes 30 **per fritter** 1.8g total fat (0.3g saturated fat); 130kJ (31 cal); 0.2g carbohydrate; 3.7g protein; 0.1g fibre
per teaspoon sauce 0g total fat (0g saturated fat); 8kJ (2 cal); 0.5g carbohydrate; 0.1g protein; 0g fibre
tips to save time, buy 400g of shelled uncooked prawns. If you can't find a kaffir lime leaf, just use 1 teaspoon of finely grated lime rind.

Skewered lemon prawns

Soak bamboo skewers in cold water for at least an hour prior to use, to prevent splintering or scorching.

1.5kg uncooked large king prawns
¼ cup (60ml) olive oil
1 tablespoon grated lemon rind
freshly ground black pepper

1 Remove heads and legs from prawns, leaving shells intact. Cut along the length of the prawn on the underside, without cutting all the way through. Thread prawns onto skewers.
2 Place prawns in shallow dish; pour over combined oil and rind. Sprinkle with pepper.
3 Cook prawns on heated grill plate (or grill or barbecue), flesh-side down, until browned lightly. Turn; cook until just cooked through.
4 Serve with lemon wedges, if desired.

on the table in 20 minutes
serves 8 **per serving** 7.4g total fat (1.1g saturated fat); 602kJ (144 cal); 0.1g carbohydrate; 19.2g protein; 0.1g fibre

Grilled swordfish and snow pea skewers

You need 24 bamboo skewers; soak them in cold water for at least an hour prior to use, to prevent splintering or scorching.

400g swordfish steak
24 large snow peas (120g)
2 teaspoons Tabasco sauce
¼ cup (60ml) lemon juice
2 tablespoons olive oil

1 Remove skin and bones from fish; cut fish into 24 long thin slices. Thread each slice, with one snow pea, on a skewer; brush with half of the combined remaining ingredients.
2 Cook skewers, in batches, on heated oiled grill plate (or grill or barbecue), brushing constantly with remaining Tabasco mixture, until fish is browned lightly and cooked as desired. Serve hot.

on the table in 30 minutes
makes 24 **per skewer** 1.9g total fat (0.3g saturated fat); 138kJ (33 cal); 0.4g carbohydrate; 3.6g protein; 0.1g fibre
tip uncooked fish and snow peas can be skewered up to 4 hours ahead. Cover; refrigerate until required.

Tuna and fetta turnovers

425g can tuna in oil
100g ricotta cheese
100g fetta cheese, crumbled
50g sun-dried tomatoes, sliced thinly
2 teaspoons drained baby capers
2 tablespoons finely chopped fresh flat-leaf parsley
2 tablespoons toasted pine nuts
1 tablespoon lemon juice
4 sheets ready-rolled puff pastry, thawed
2 tablespoons milk

1 Preheat oven to 200°C/180°C fan-forced. Oil oven trays.
2 Drain tuna over small bowl, reserving 2 tablespoons of the tuna oil.
Flake tuna into medium bowl, add cheeses, tomatoes, capers, parsley,
nuts, juice and reserved tuna oil; mix well.
3 Cut four 12cm rounds from each pastry sheet. Place one heaped
tablespoon of tuna mixture on each round; brush edges with a little milk,
fold over to enclose filling. Press edges to seal; repeat with remaining
tuna mixture and pastry.
4 Place turnovers on trays; brush lightly with milk. Bake, uncovered,
about 15 minutes or until browned lightly.

on the table in 35 minutes
makes 16 **per turnover** 18.2g total fat (7.3g saturated fat); 1137kJ
(272 cal); 17.2g carbohydrate; 9.5g protein; 1.2g fibre

Salt, pepper and paprika prawns

24 uncooked medium king prawns (1kg)
2 teaspoons sweet paprika
2 teaspoons sea salt
1 teaspoon cracked black pepper
lemon yogurt dip
⅓ cup (95g) greek-style yogurt
1 clove garlic, crushed
1 tablespoon lemon juice

1 Shell and devein prawns, leaving tails intact. Combine prawns with paprika, salt and pepper in medium bowl.
2 Make lemon yogurt dip.
3 Cook prawns, in batches, on heated oiled grill plate (or grill or barbecue) until changed in colour.
4 Serve prawns with dip.
lemon yogurt dip combine ingredients in small bowl.

on the table in 25 minutes
makes 24 **per prawn** 0.4g total fat (0.2g saturated fat); 100kJ (24 cal); 0.4g carbohydrate; 4.5g protein; 0g fibre

Mussels with chilli-lime sauce

32 large black mussels (1.6kg)
1 cup (250ml) water
¼ cup (60ml) sweet chilli sauce
1 tablespoon tequila
⅓ cup (80ml) lime juice
1 tablespoon finely chopped fresh coriander

1 Scrub mussels; remove beards.
2 Bring the water to a boil in medium saucepan; cook mussels, covered, about 5 minutes or until mussels open (discard any that do not). Drain; discard liquid. Break open shells; discard tops. Loosen mussels from bottom shells with a spoon; place mussels in shells, in single layer, on serving platter. Cover; refrigerate 15 minutes or until cold.
3 Combine remaining ingredients in medium jug; divide chilli-lime mixture among mussels. Serve cold.

on the table in 35 minutes
makes 32 **per mussel** 0.1g total fat (0g saturated fat); 38kJ (9 cal); 0.9g carbohydrate; 0.6g protein; 0.1g fibre
tip use a stiff brush to scrub the mussels under cold water. Chilli-lime sauce can be made a day ahead. Cover; refrigerate until required.

Five-spice calamari

1kg whole small calamari
½ cup (75g) plain flour
¼ cup (55g) crushed sea salt flakes or 1 tablespoon sea salt
1½ tablespoons ground white pepper
1 tablespoon five-spice powder
1½ teaspoons chilli powder
vegetable oil, for deep-frying

1 Clean calamari by gently pulling head and tentacles away from body.
Remove clear backbone (quill) from inside body. Cut tentacles from head
just below eyes; discard head. Remove side fins and skin from body with
salted fingers. Rinse body, tentacles and fins if necessary.
2 Cut body to open out flat. Using a sharp knife, lightly score inside flesh
in a diagonal pattern. Cut tentacles into pieces and fins into strips. Pat
calamari dry on absorbent paper.
3 Combine flour, salt, pepper, five-spice and chilli in large bowl.
4 Add a small handful of calamari to flour mixture and toss to coat.
Deep-fry calamari in hot oil until browned lightly and crisp. Drain well on
absorbent paper. Repeat with remaining calamari and flour mixture.

on the table in 25 minutes
serves 4 **per serving** 7g total fat (1.2g saturated fat); 860kJ (205 cal);
14.2g carbohydrate; 20.2g protein; 1.4g fibre
tip calamari is best eaten as soon as it is cooked, but can be kept
warm, on an absorbent-paper-lined tray, in a very slow oven while
cooking in batches.

Thai fish cakes

500g skinless redfish fillets, boned, chopped coarsely
2 tablespoons red curry paste
2 fresh kaffir lime leaves, torn
2 green onions, chopped coarsely
1 tablespoon fish sauce
1 tablespoon lime juice
2 tablespoons finely chopped fresh coriander
3 snake beans (30g), chopped finely
2 fresh small red thai chillies, chopped finely
peanut oil, for deep-frying
cucumber dipping sauce
1 lebanese cucumber (130g), seeded, sliced thinly
½ cup (110g) white sugar
1 cup (250ml) water
½ cup (125ml) white vinegar
4cm piece fresh ginger (20g), grated
1 teaspoon salt
2 fresh small red thai chillies, sliced thinly
3 green onions, sliced thinly
1 tablespoon coarsely chopped fresh coriander

1 Make cucumber dipping sauce.
2 Blend or process fish with paste, lime leaves, onion, sauce and juice until mixture forms a smooth paste. Combine fish mixture in medium bowl with coriander, beans and chilli.
3 Roll heaped tablespoons of mixture into balls with wet hands; flatten balls into cake shape.
4 Heat oil in wok; deep-fry fish cakes, in batches, until browned lightly and cooked through. Drain on absorbent paper; serve with dipping sauce and lime wedges, if desired.
cucumber dipping sauce place cucumber in heatproof serving bowl. Stir sugar, the water, vinegar, ginger and salt in small saucepan over heat without boiling until sugar is dissolved; pour over cucumber. Sprinkle with chilli, onion and coriander; refrigerate until required.

on the table in 35 minutes
makes 16 **per fish cake** 3.7g total fat (0.7g saturated fat); 263kJ (63 cal); 0.4g carbohydrate; 6.7g protein; 0.4g fibre

Spicy prawns

18 uncooked medium king prawns (810g)
2 cloves garlic, crushed
1 fresh long red chilli, chopped finely
2 tablespoons olive oil
1 tablespoon lemon juice

1 Shell and devein prawns, leaving tails intact.
2 Combine prawns, garlic, chilli and oil in medium bowl.
3 Cook prawns in large heated frying pan, in batches, until just changed in colour. Serve prawns drizzled with juice.

on the table in 25 minutes
serves 6 **per serving** 6.5g total fat (0.9g saturated fat); 481kJ (115 cal); 0.2g carbohydrate; 13.9g protein; 0.2g fibre

Scallops st jacques-style

You need 24 Chinese porcelain spoons for serving.

24 scallops (600g), roe removed
½ cup (125ml) dry white wine
½ cup (125ml) cream
1 tablespoon fresh chervil leaves

1 Rinse scallops under cold water. Dry scallops on absorbent paper.
2 Bring wine to a boil in medium frying pan; reduce heat, then simmer until reduced by half. Whisk in cream; bring to a boil. Reduce heat, simmer, uncovered, about 5 minutes or until liquid has reduced by two-thirds. Add scallops; cook 1 minute. Remove from heat.
3 Place one scallop on each spoon; place on serving tray before spooning sauce over each scallop. Top with chervil leaves. Serve hot.

on the table in 20 minutes
makes 24 **per spoon** 2.4g total fat (1.5g saturated fat); 159kJ (38 cal); 0.3g carbohydrate; 3g protein; 0g fibre
tip scallops can be cleaned up to 4 hours ahead. Cover; refrigerate until required.

Smoked salmon with avocado salsa and prawns

24 slices smoked salmon (400g)
16 cooked medium king prawns (560g)
1 tablespoon salmon roe
8 fresh dill sprigs
avocado salsa
2 medium egg tomatoes (150g), seeded, chopped finely
2 small avocados (400g), chopped finely
½ small red onion (50g), chopped finely
1 tablespoon finely chopped fresh chives
2 teaspoons finely chopped fresh dill
1 teaspoon finely grated lemon rind
2 tablespoons lemon juice
lemon chive dressing
¼ cup (60ml) olive oil
2 tablespoons lemon juice
1 tablespoon finely chopped fresh chives

1 Make avocado salsa and lemon chive dressing.
2 Line eight holes of a 12-hole (⅓-cup/80ml) muffin pan with plastic wrap, bringing the plastic 3cm above the edge of the holes.
3 Place one salmon slice in base of each muffin hole; fold over excess. Top each slice with 2 tablespoons of the salsa; lay another slice of salmon in each hole. Repeat layers with salsa and salmon slices. Fold over plastic to seal; refrigerate until required.
4 Shell and devein prawns, leaving tails intact.
5 Turn out salmon parcels; unwrap. Divide parcels among serving plates; top with prawns, roe and dill, drizzle with dressing.
avocado salsa combine ingredients in small bowl.
lemon chive dressing place ingredients in screw-top jar; shake well.

on the table in 35 minutes
serves 8 **per serving** 17.5g total fat (3.2g saturated fat); 1016kJ (243 cal); 1.2g carbohydrate; 20.1g protein; 0.9g fibre

Prawn cocktail with lime aïoli

A modern take on the traditional prawn cocktail, this version uses baby rocket leaves rather than iceberg lettuce and replaces bottled cocktail sauce with aïoli – a light and zesty garlic and lime mayonnaise.

40 medium cooked prawns (1.4kg)
100g baby rocket leaves
lime aïoli
½ cup (150g) mayonnaise
2 teaspoons finely grated lime rind
2 tablespoons lime juice
2 cloves garlic, crushed
1 fresh small red thai chilli, sliced thinly

1 Make lime aïoli.
2 Shell and devein prawns, leaving tails intact.
3 Place prawns in large bowl with rocket, toss gently to combine.
4 Divide prawn salad among serving dishes; spoon aïoli evenly on top.
lime aïoli combine ingredients in small bowl.

on the table in 20 minutes
serves 4 **per serving** 13.4g total fat (1.5g saturated fat); 1275kJ (305 cal); 8.4g carbohydrate; 37.1g protein; 0.9g fibre
tips you can assemble the aïoli early on the day you intend to serve it and refrigerate, covered. Similarly, if you shell and devein the prawns and store them in a small glass bowl, covered, in the refrigerator early on the day, then it's just a simple matter of tossing them with the rocket and dolloping on the aioli at mealtime.

Scallop and lime mini kebabs

24 scallops (600g), roe removed
2 tablespoons vegetable oil
4cm piece fresh ginger (20g), grated
3 cloves garlic, crushed
3 limes
12 fresh kaffir lime leaves, halved lengthways
24 sturdy toothpicks

1 Combine scallops, oil, ginger and garlic in medium bowl.
Cover; refrigerate 15 minutes.
2 Meanwhile, cut each lime into eight wedges. Skewer one lime
wedge and one piece of lime leaf onto each toothpick.
3 Cook scallops on oiled grill plate (or grill or barbecue) about
5 minutes or until cooked as desired. Skewer one scallop onto
each toothpick.

on the table in 35 minutes
makes 24 **per kebab** 1.7g total fat (0.2g saturated fat); 121kJ (29 cal);
0.3g carbohydrate; 3g protein; 0.2g fibre

Bloody mary oyster shots

You need 16 shot glasses for this recipe.

16 oysters
2 tablespoons vodka
2 tablespoons lemon juice
¾ cup (180ml) tomato juice
¼ teaspoon Tabasco sauce
1 teaspoon worcestershire sauce

1 Place one oyster in each glass.
2 Combine remaining ingredients in medium jug; divide mixture among glasses. Serve cold.

on the table in 10 minutes
makes 16 **per shot** 0.2g total fat (0g saturated fat); 67kJ (16 cal); 0.7g carbohydrate; 1.3g protein; 0.1g fibre
tip bloody mary mixture can be made a day ahead. Cover; refrigerate until required.

Steamed scallops with asian flavours

1½ cups (300g) jasmine rice
3cm piece fresh ginger (15g)
20 scallops (800g), in half shell, roe removed
2 tablespoons thinly sliced fresh lemon grass
4 green onions, sliced thinly
1 tablespoon sesame oil
¼ cup (60ml) kecap manis
¼ cup (60ml) soy sauce

1 Cook rice in large saucepan of boiling water, uncovered, until just tender; drain.
2 Meanwhile, slice ginger thinly; cut slices into thin strips. Place scallops, in batches, in single layer in large bamboo steamer; top with ginger, lemon grass and onion. Cover; steam about 5 minutes or until scallops are tender and cooked as desired.
3 Divide scallops among serving plates; top with combined remaining ingredients. Serve with rice.

on the table in 30 minutes
serves 4 **per serving** 5.5g total fat (0.9g saturated fat); 1517kJ (363 cal); 61.2g carbohydrate; 15.8g protein; 0.9g fibre
tip you can also use scallops with the roe attached, if you prefer.

Smoked trout pâté

400g whole smoked trout
1 egg yolk
2 teaspoons white vinegar
2 teaspoons mustard powder
1 tablespoon lemon juice
¼ teaspoon lemon pepper seasoning
⅓ cup (80ml) extra light olive oil

1 Remove skin and bones from trout; coarsely flake flesh.
2 Blend or process egg yolk, vinegar, mustard, juice and lemon pepper until smooth. With motor operating, add oil gradually in a thin stream. Add trout; blend until smooth.

on the table in 20 minutes
serves 4 **per serving** 22.3g total fat (3.6g saturated fat); 1068kJ (255 cal); 0.1g carbohydrate; 14.1g protein; 0g fibre

Crab rice paper rolls

You need to buy half a small wombok for this recipe.

½ cup (125ml) mirin
⅓ cup (80ml) soy sauce
2 teaspoons fish sauce
2 teaspoons sesame oil
⅓ cup (80ml) lime juice
1 tablespoon white sugar
⅓ cup finely chopped fresh coriander
500g cooked crab meat
2 cups (160g) finely shredded wombok
½ cup coarsely chopped fresh mint
1 medium carrot (120g), cut into matchsticks
1½ cups (120g) bean sprouts
1 cup (50g) snow pea sprouts
1 fresh small red thai chilli, chopped finely
20 x 16cm-round rice paper sheets

1 Combine mirin, sauces, oil, juice, sugar and coriander in small jug. Place crab in medium bowl with half of the mirin mixture; toss gently to combine.
2 Combine wombok, mint, carrot, sprouts and chilli in large bowl.
3 Place 1 sheet of rice paper in medium bowl of warm water until just softened; lift from water carefully, place on board covered with tea towel. Place about ¼ cup of the wombok mixture in centre of rice paper, top with about 1 tablespoon of the crab mixture. Fold in two opposing sides; roll to enclose filling. Repeat with remaining rice paper sheets, wombok mixture and crab mixture.
4 Serve rolls with remaining mirin mixture as a dipping sauce.

on the table in 35 minutes
makes 20 **per roll** 0.8g total fat (0.1g saturated fat); 493kJ (118 cal); 10.9g carbohydrate; 11.4g protein; 9g fibre
tip lobster or prawn meat can be substituted for the crab, if desired.

Oysters with lime and coriander

24 oysters, on the half shell
¼ cup (60ml) lime juice
1 teaspoon Tabasco sauce
2 tablespoons coarsely chopped fresh coriander
2 green onions, sliced thinly
1 tablespoon peanut oil
1 clove garlic, crushed
1 teaspoon brown sugar

1 Carefully remove oysters from shells; wash and dry shells. Return oysters to shells; place, in single layer, on serving platter.
2 Place remaining ingredients in screw-top jar; shake well. Divide dressing among oysters.

on the table in 10 minutes
makes 24 **per oyster** 1g total fat (0.2g saturated fat); 67kJ (16 cal); 0.3g carbohydrate; 1.3g protein; 0.1g fibre
tip dressing can be made a day ahead. Refrigerate until required.

Prawns with rocket pistou

1kg cooked medium prawns
1 clove garlic
1½ cups loosely packed baby rocket leaves
1 tablespoon grated parmesan cheese
2 tablespoons olive oil
1 teaspoon lemon juice, approximately

1 Shell and devein prawns, leaving tails intact.
2 Blend or process garlic and rocket until rocket is chopped, add cheese. With motor operating, gradually pour in oil, in a thin steam, until combined.
3 Transfer pistou to small bowl, add juice; cover surface with plastic wrap until ready to serve, to prevent discolouration.
4 Serve prawns with pistou.

on the table in 20 minutes
serves 4 **per serving** 10.6g total fat (1.8g saturated fat); 861kJ (206 cal); 0.6g carbohydrate; 26.9g protein; 0.5g fibre
tip rocket pistou can be made up to eight hours ahead. For a milder pistou, substitute flat-leaf parsley for half of the rocket.

Tuna dip

180g can sandwich tuna in oil
½ small white onion (40g), chopped finely
30g soft butter
1 teaspoon grated lemon rind
2 teaspoons lemon juice
1 clove garlic, crushed
2 teaspoons drained capers, chopped
1 tablespoon chopped fresh basil
2 teaspoons chopped fresh oregano

1 Blend or process undrained tuna, onion, butter, rind, juice and garlic until smooth; transfer mixture to medium bowl.
2 Add capers and herbs to tuna mixture; mix well.
3 Serve with fresh crusty bread, if desired.

on the table in 10 minutes
makes 1¼ cups **per tablespoon** 4.4g total fat (1.5g saturated fat);
213kJ (51 cal); 0.2g carbohydrate; 2.6g protein; 0.1g fibre
tip dip can be made up to 4 hours ahead. Cover; refrigerate until required.

salads

Prawn and avocado salad with ginger dressing

1kg cooked medium king prawns
200g snow peas, trimmed, sliced thinly
1 bunch fresh chives, cut into 4cm lengths
100g baby spinach leaves
1 medium avocado (250g), sliced thickly
ginger dressing
12cm piece fresh ginger (60g), grated
2 tablespoons olive oil
2 tablespoons lemon juice
1 teaspoon white sugar

1 Shell and devein prawns; cut prawns in half lengthways.
2 Make ginger dressing.
3 Place prawns in large bowl with snow peas, chives, spinach, avocado and dressing; toss gently to combine.
ginger dressing press grated ginger between two spoons over screw-top jar; discard fibres. Add remaining ingredients; shake well.

on the table in 35 minutes
serves 4 **per serving** 20.1g total fat (3.6g saturated fat); 1329kJ (318 cal); 5.2g carbohydrate; 29.1g protein; 3.5g fibre

Niçoise salad

The original "salade niçoise", from the French Mediterranean city of Nice, was made of the best of that region's produce: ripe vine tomatoes, local capers, hand-picked baby beans, tiny dark brown olives, anchovies and tuna fresh from the sea, and plump cloves of garlic. No wonder it so delighted foreign visitors to Nice that they took the memory of that salad to all corners of the globe, adapting it slightly, as we have here, to suit their own produce and lifestyle.

3 x 125g cans tuna slices in springwater, drained
1 medium red onion (170g), sliced thinly
250g baby spinach leaves, trimmed
300g can white beans, rinsed, drained
150g yellow teardrop tomatoes, halved
½ cup (80g) kalamata olives, seeded
4 hard-boiled eggs, quartered
dressing
½ cup (125ml) olive oil
¼ cup (60ml) lemon juice
1 clove garlic, crushed
1 teaspoon coarsely chopped fresh lemon thyme
2 teaspoons dijon mustard
¼ teaspoon white sugar

1 Make dressing.
2 Place tuna, onion, spinach, beans, tomato, olives and egg in large bowl with dressing; toss gently to combine.
dressing place ingredients in screw-top jar; shake well.

on the table in 10 minutes
serves 4 **per serving** 36.3g total fat (6.4g saturated fat); 2132kJ (510 cal); 13.1g carbohydrate; 30.8g protein; 5.6g fibre
tip if you gently stir the eggs until they begin to boil, you will have nicely centred yolks, a good look when they're to be served quartered, as they are here.

Seared scallops with mixed cabbage salad

32 scallops (1.3kg), roe removed
2 lebanese cucumbers (260g)
3 cups (240g) finely shredded red cabbage
2 cups (160g) finely shredded savoy cabbage
½ cup coarsely chopped fresh chives
2 tablespoons toasted sesame seeds
honey soy dressing
2 tablespoons soy sauce
2 tablespoons lemon juice
2 teaspoons sesame oil
1 tablespoon honey
1 clove garlic, crushed
¼ cup (60ml) peanut oil

1 Make honey soy dressing.
2 Sear scallops in large heated oiled frying pan, in batches, until browned both sides and cooked as desired.
3 Using vegetable peeler, slice cucumbers into ribbons. Place cucumber in large bowl with cabbages, chives, seeds and three-quarters of the dressing; toss gently to combine.
4 Divide salad among serving plates; top with scallops, drizzle with remaining dressing.
honey soy dressing place ingredients in screw-top jar; shake well.

on the table in 25 minutes
serves 4 **per serving** 20.8g total fat (3.6g saturated fat); 1480kJ (354 cal); 12g carbohydrate; 27.5g protein; 5.3g fibre
tip for this recipe, you need approximately half a medium red cabbage and a quarter of a medium savoy cabbage.

Smoked trout and potato salad with yogurt dressing

700g kipfler potatoes
1 cup (280g) yogurt
1 tablespoon wholegrain mustard
2 tablespoons finely chopped fresh dill
2 tablespoons finely chopped fresh chives
2 tablespoons cornichons (small gherkins), chopped finely
400g smoked trout, boned, flaked
50g watercress

1 Boil, steam or microwave potatoes until tender; drain. Cool; slice thickly.
2 Meanwhile, combine yogurt, mustard, herbs and cornichons in large bowl. Stir through potatoes.
3 To serve, divide potato salad among plates, top with trout and watercress.

on the table in 35 minutes
serves 4 **per serving** 7.7g total fat (2.7g saturated fat); 1359kJ (325 cal); 28.6g carbohydrate; 33g protein; 4g fibre

Prawn, papaya and green apple salad

1kg cooked medium king prawns
1 small daikon (400g)
2 small green apples (260g), sliced thinly
1 medium red onion (170g), sliced thinly
1 small papaya (650g), cut into 1.5cm pieces
1 small honeydew melon (900g), diced into 1.5cm pieces
400g watercress, trimmed
wasabi dressing
2 tablespoons apple cider vinegar
1 teaspoon wasabi paste
1 clove garlic, crushed
1 tablespoon lemon juice
¼ cup (60ml) olive oil

1 Shell and devein prawns, leaving tails intact.
2 Make wasabi dressing.
3 Slice radish thinly; cut slices into matchstick-sized pieces. Place in large bowl with apple, onion, papaya, melon and dressing; toss gently to combine.
4 Divide watercress among serving plates; top with salad then prawns.
wasabi dressing place ingredients in screw-top jar; shake well.

on the table in 25 minutes
serves 4 **per serving** 16.6g total fat (2.1g saturated fat); 1659kJ (397 cal); 29g carbohydrate; 30.3g protein; 9.4g fibre
tips a fairly hard, unripe papaya is ideal for this recipe but if none is available, buy the firmest ripe papaya you can find. We used unpeeled granny smith apples in this recipe, both for their crisp tartness and pale green peel. Use a mandoline or V-slicer, if you own one or the other, to slice the daikon and apple as thinly as possible. This recipe should not be made until just before serving to avoid discolouration of the fruit.

Char-grilled cuttlefish, rocket and parmesan salad

1kg cuttlefish hoods
2 tablespoons olive oil
1 tablespoon finely grated lemon rind
⅓ cup (80ml) lemon juice
1 clove garlic, crushed
150g rocket
150g semi-dried tomatoes, drained, chopped coarsely
1 small red onion (100g), sliced thinly
1 tablespoon drained baby capers, rinsed
80g parmesan cheese, shaved
2 tablespoons balsamic vinegar
⅓ cup (80ml) olive oil, extra

1 Halve cuttlefish lengthways, score insides in crosshatch pattern then cut into 5cm strips. Combine cuttlefish in medium bowl with oil, rind, juice and garlic. Cover; refrigerate 5 minutes.
2 Meanwhile, combine rocket, tomato, onion, capers and cheese in large bowl.
3 Drain cuttlefish; discard marinade. Cook cuttlefish, in batches, on heated oiled grill plate (or grill or barbecue) until cooked through.
4 Add cuttlefish to salad with combined vinegar and extra oil; toss gently to combine.

on the table in 35 minutes
serves 4 **per serving** 37.3g total fat (8.2g saturated fat); 2228kJ (533 cal); 16.5g carbohydrate; 30.5g protein; 6.7g fibre

Warm tuna salad with lemon and dill dressing

1 tablespoon olive oil
1 medium white onion (150g), sliced thinly
1 clove garlic, crushed
250g cherry tomatoes, halved
300g can chickpeas, rinsed, drained
500g frozen broad beans, thawed, peeled
100g rocket leaves
2 tablespoons fresh dill sprigs
425g can tuna, drained, flaked
lemon and dill dressing
⅓ cup (100g) lemon and dill mayonnaise
2 tablespoons olive oil
2 tablespoons lemon juice
1 teaspoon white sugar

1 Make lemon and dill dressing.
2 Heat oil in large frying pan, add onion, cook, stirring, until soft.
Add garlic, tomatoes, chickpeas and broad beans; stir until hot.
3 Place mixture in bowl with rocket leaves and dill; toss gently.
4 Divide salad among serving plates, top with tuna and lemon and dill dressing.
lemon and dill dressing combine all ingredients in small bowl.

on the table in 30 minutes
serves 4 **per serving** 25.9g total fat (4g saturated fat); 1944kJ (465 cal); 18.9g carbohydrate; 34g protein; 11.4g fibre
tip lemon and dill dressing can be made a day ahead. Cover; refrigerate until required. Recipe best made just before serving.

Salmon pasta salad with lemon mayonnaise

250g orecchiette pasta
20 drained caperberries (100g)
2 x 400g cans red salmon, drained, flaked
1 large white onion (200g), halved, sliced thinly
4 trimmed celery stalks (400g), sliced thinly
4 large red cabbage leaves, trimmed
lemon mayonnaise
2 tablespoons water
⅔ cup (200g) mayonnaise
½ cup (120g) sour cream
¼ cup (60ml) lemon juice
¼ cup coarsely chopped fresh dill

1 Cook pasta in large saucepan of boiling water, uncovered, until just tender; drain. Rinse under cold water; drain
2 Meanwhile, make lemon mayonnaise.
3 Slice eight of the caperberries thinly. Place sliced caperberries in large bowl with salmon, onion, celery, pasta and half of the mayonnaise; toss gently to combine.
4 Divide cabbage among serving bowls; fill with salad, top with remaining mayonnaise and remaining caperberries.
lemon mayonnaise whisk ingredients in small bowl until well combined.

on the table in 25 minutes
serves 4 **per serving** 48.5g total fat (15.1g saturated fat); 3641kJ (871 cal); 60.6g carbohydrate; 45.7g protein; 6.1g fibre
tip orecchiette is a bite-sized pasta, perfectly shaped to hold chunky vegetables in sauces or salads. It has a slightly different taste and texture to others, as it's made with a custom blend of durum wheat semolina.

Tuna, bean and tomato salad

185g can tuna in springwater, drained, flaked
300g can red kidney beans, drained, rinsed
1 small red onion (100g), sliced thinly
250g cherry tomatoes, halved
½ cup coarsely chopped fresh basil
1 medium avocado (250g), sliced thickly
100g baby rocket leaves
balsamic dressing
2 tablespoons olive oil
1 tablespoon balsamic vinegar
1 teaspoon finely grated lemon rind
1 tablespoon lemon juice
1 teaspoon dijon mustard
1 clove garlic, crushed

1 Make balsamic dressing.
2 Place ingredients in large bowl with dressing; toss gently to combine.
balsamic dressing place ingredients in screw-top jar; shake well.

on the table in 10 minutes
serves 4 **per serving** 20.6g total fat (3.9g saturated fat); 1204kJ
(288 cal); 10.6g carbohydrate; 15g protein; 6g fibre

Grilled octopus salad

600g cleaned baby octopus
1 cup (150g) seeded kalamata olives
5 lebanese cucumbers (650g), seeded, chopped coarsely
200g grape tomatoes, halved
⅓ cup coarsely chopped fresh flat-leaf parsley
dressing
⅓ cup (80ml) orange juice
1 tablespoon lemon juice
⅔ cup (160ml) olive oil
1 clove garlic, crushed

1 Make dressing.
2 Cook octopus, in batches, on heated oiled grill plate (or grill or barbecue) until cooked as desired.
3 Combine octopus and dressing in medium bowl. Add olives, cucumber, tomato and parsley; toss gently to combine
dressing place ingredients in screw-top jar; shake well.

on the table in 20 minutes
serves 4 **per serving** 38.1g total fat (5.2g saturated fat); 2107kJ
(504 cal); 13.7g carbohydrate; 26g protein; 3g fibre

Chilli tuna pasta salad

300g large shell pasta
250g fresh green beans, trimmed, halved
2 x 185g cans tuna in chilli oil
⅓ cup coarsely chopped fresh flat-leaf parsley
⅓ cup firmly packed fresh basil leaves, torn
2 tablespoons drained baby capers
150g baby rocket leaves
¼ cup (60ml) olive oil
¼ cup (60ml) lemon juice
2 cloves garlic, crushed
2 teaspoons white sugar

1 Cook pasta in large saucepan of boiling water, uncovered, until just tender; drain. Rinse under cold water; drain.
2 Meanwhile, boil, steam or microwave beans until just tender; drain. Rinse under cold water; drain.
3 Drain tuna; reserve oil. Place tuna in large bowl; flake with fork. Add pasta and beans with herbs, capers and rocket; toss gently to combine.
4 Place remaining ingredients and reserved oil in screw-top jar; shake well. Drizzle dressing over salad; toss gently to combine.

on the table in 30 minutes
serves 6 **per serving** 17g total fat (2.5g saturated fat); 1659kJ (397 cal); 38.9g carbohydrate; 20.4g protein; 3.3g fibre
tips the salad, without the dressing, can be made several hours ahead and refrigerated, covered. Toss the dressing through the salad just before serving. For an even more Mediterranean touch, add about 200g of diced fetta cheese to the salad.

Hot and sour prawn vermicelli salad

1kg cooked medium king prawns
250g dried rice vermicelli noodles
1 lime
1 lemon
1 medium red capsicum (200g), sliced thinly
1 medium yellow capsicum (200g), sliced thinly
1 medium red onion (170g), sliced thinly
¼ cup (60ml) olive oil
¼ cup (60ml) rice vinegar
1 tablespoon sambal oelek
1 tablespoon fish sauce
2 tablespoons grated palm sugar
1 cup firmly packed fresh coriander leaves

1 Shell and devein prawns, leaving tails intact.
2 Place noodles in large heatproof bowl of boiling water, stand until just tender; drain. Rinse under cold water; drain.
3 Meanwhile, halve lime and lemon lengthways; slice 1 unpeeled half of each thinly, place in large bowl. Squeeze remaining halves over bowl; add prawns, noodles and remaining ingredients, toss gently to combine.

on the table in 35 minutes
serves 4 **per serving** 15.4g total fat (2.1g saturated fat); 2057kJ (492 cal); 53.5g carbohydrate; 32.3g protein; 3.5g fibre

Crab and apple salad

250g sugar snap peas, trimmed
1 large apple (200g)
500g cooked crab meat
1 medium red onion (170g), halved, sliced thinly
2 fresh small red thai chillies, sliced thinly lengthways
2 medium avocados (500g), sliced thickly
150g mesclun
dressing
⅓ cup (80ml) olive oil
¼ cup (60ml) lemon juice
1 tablespoon dijon mustard
1 clove garlic, crushed

1 Boil, steam or microwave peas until just tender; drain. Rinse under cold water; drain.
2 Meanwhile, make dressing.
3 Slice apple thinly; cut slices into thin strips.
4 Combine peas and apple in large bowl with crab, onion, chilli, avocado, mesclun and dressing; toss gently to combine.
dressing place ingredients in screw-top jar; shake well.

on the table in 25 minutes
serves 4 **per serving** 39.3g total fat (7g saturated fat); 3057kJ (492 cal); 12.5g carbohydrate; 20.9g protein; 5.1g fibre

Smoked trout and crisp noodle salad

450g smoked ocean trout fillets
3½ cups (280g) finely shredded red cabbage
2 medium carrots (240g), grated coarsely
2 x 100g packets fried noodles
4 green onions, sliced thinly
2 tablespoons toasted sesame seeds
dressing
½ cup (125ml) sweet chilli sauce
1 tablespoon sesame oil
2 tablespoons white wine vinegar
2 tablespoons soy sauce

1 Make dressing.
2 Discard any skin and bones from fish. Flake fish in large bowl; add cabbage, carrot, noodles, onion and seeds.
3 Pour dressing over salad; toss gently to combine.
dressing place ingredients in screw-top jar; shake well.

on the table in 25 minutes
serves 4 **per serving** 20.8g total fat (5.4g saturated fat); 1810kJ (433 cal); 23.3g carbohydrate; 34.8g protein; 7.3g fibre
tips filleted portions of smoked trout, in a variety of sizes, are now available at most supermarkets; we used three 150g portions for this recipe. Fried noodles are crisp wheat noodles packaged (commonly in 100g packets) already deep-fried. You need a quarter of a medium red cabbage, about 375g, for this recipe.

Prawn, endive and pink grapefruit with lime aïoli

3 small pink grapefruits (1kg)
1kg cooked medium king prawns
350g curly endive, torn
¼ cup coarsely chopped fresh chives
2 trimmed celery stalks (200g), sliced thinly
1 small red onion (100g), sliced thinly
lime aïoli
2 egg yolks
2 teaspoons dijon mustard
½ teaspoon finely grated lime rind
2 tablespoons lime juice
2 cloves garlic, quartered
¾ cup (180ml) light olive oil
1 tablespoon hot water

1 Make lime aïoli.
2 Peel grapefruits; separate the segments. Shell and devein prawns, leaving tails intact.
3 Combine grapefruit and prawns in large serving bowl with remaining ingredients. Serve with lime aïoli.
lime aïoli blend or process egg yolks, mustard, rind, juice and garlic until combined. With motor operating, gradually add oil, blending until aïoli thickens. With motor operating, add enough of the water (if any) to achieve desired consistency.

on the table in 30 minutes
serves 4 **per serving** 8.9g total fat (1.3g saturated fat); 472kJ (113 cal); 2.1g carbohydrate; 6.1g protein; 0.9g fibre
tip lime aïoli can be prepared a day ahead. Cover; refrigerate until required.

Warm salmon, risoni and pea salad

250g risoni pasta
2 cups (240g) frozen peas
1 tablespoon olive oil
500g salmon fillets
8 green onions, sliced thickly
100g baby spinach leaves
dill dressing
2 tablespoons olive oil
2 teaspoons finely grated lemon rind
¼ cup (60ml) lemon juice
1 teaspoon dijon mustard
1 tablespoon coarsely chopped fresh dill

1 Cook pasta in large saucepan of boiling water, uncovered, until almost tender. Add peas to pan with pasta and cook until peas and pasta are just tender; drain.
2 Meanwhile, make dill dressing.
3 Heat oil in large frying pan; cook fish, uncovered, until cooked as desired. Remove from pan; stand 5 minutes. Discard skin and any bones. Flake fish into large chunks.
4 Place pasta, peas and fish in large bowl with onion, spinach and dressing; toss gently to combine.
dill dressing place ingredients in screw-top jar; shake well.

on the table in 25 minutes
serves 4 **per serving** 23.6g total fat (4.1g saturated fat); 2324kJ
(556 cal); 49g carbohydrate; 3.6g protein; 7.8g fibre

Tuna and white bean salad with french dressing

2 trimmed celery stalks (200g)
2 x 425g cans tuna chunks in brine, drained, flaked
400g can white beans, rinsed, drained
1 medium red onion (170g), sliced thinly
1 cup (150g) seeded kalamata olives
1 medium red capsicum (200g), sliced thinly
1 cup firmly packed fresh flat-leaf parsley leaves
french dressing
1 clove garlic, crushed
⅓ cup (80ml) lemon juice
⅓ cup (80ml) olive oil

1 Make french dressing.
2 Cut celery into 5cm pieces; cut pieces into thin strips lengthways.
3 Combine celery in large bowl with remaining ingredients and dressing; toss gently to combine.
french dressing place ingredients in screw-top jar; shake well.

on the table in 15 minutes
serves 4 **per serving** 23.5g total fat (4.4g saturated fat); 2086kJ (499 cal); 20g carbohydrate; 48.7g protein; 6.8g fibre
tip many varieties of already cooked white beans are available canned, among them cannellini, butter and haricot beans; any of these are suitable for this salad.

Thai-style salmon salad with lime dressing

400g can red salmon, drained
1 lebanese cucumber (130g), sliced
4 large shallots (100g), sliced
200g cherry tomatoes, halved
2 baby cos lettuce
8 mint leaves
8 basil leaves, torn
lime dressing
¼ cup (60ml) lime juice
1 tablespoon soy sauce
1 teaspoon fish sauce
1 teaspoon brown sugar
¼ teaspoon sesame oil
1 fresh small red thai chilli, chopped finely

1 Make lime dressing.
2 Break salmon into chunks.
3 Place salmon in large bowl with remaining ingredients and dressing; toss gently to combine.
lime dressing place ingredients in screw-top jar; shake well.

on the table in 20 minutes
serves 4 **per serving** 10.5g total fat (2.7g saturated fat); 849kJ (203 cal); 5.3g carbohydrate; 20.2g protein; 3.6g fibre

Tunisian tuna salad

2 hard-boiled eggs, shelled, chopped finely
1 medium green capsicum (200g), chopped finely
2 medium tomatoes (380g), seeded, chopped finely
4 green onions, chopped finely
2 large canned anchovy fillets, drained, chopped finely
10 seeded green olives (30g), chopped finely
2 fresh small red thai chillies, chopped finely
1 tablespoon finely chopped fresh mint
180g can tuna chunks in springwater, drained, flaked
1 tablespoon drained baby capers
caraway-seed dressing
2 tablespoons olive oil
1 clove garlic, crushed
1 teaspoon coriander seeds
1 teaspoon caraway seeds
1 tablespoon lemon juice
2 tablespoons red wine vinegar

1 Make caraway-seed dressing.
2 Combine salad ingredients in medium bowl with dressing; toss gently to combine.
caraway-seed dressing heat oil in small frying pan, add garlic and seeds; cook, stirring, until fragrant. Stir in juice and vinegar.

on the table in 30 minutes
serves 4 **per serving** 13.8g total fat (2.7g saturated fat); 911kJ (218 cal); 6g carbohydrate; 16.7g protein; 2.2g fibre

Prawn and sweet chilli salad

125g dried rice vermicelli noodles
2 lebanese cucumbers (260g), seeded, cut into thin strips
2 medium carrots (240g), cut into thin strips
150g bean sprouts
500g peeled cooked medium prawns
⅓ cup firmly packed vietnamese or round mint leaves
⅓ cup firmly packed fresh coriander leaves
⅓ cup (35g) chopped roasted salted peanuts
sweet chilli dressing
⅓ cup (80ml) sweet chilli sauce
2 tablespoons fish sauce
⅓ cup (80ml) lime juice
3 fresh small red thai chillies, chopped finely

1 Place noodles in large heatproof bowl of boiling water, stand until just tender; drain. Rinse under cold water; drain.
2 Meanwhile, make sweet chilli dressing.
3 Combine noodles, cucumber, carrot, sprouts, prawns, herbs and sweet chilli dressing in large bowl; toss gently.
4 Serve sprinkled with peanuts.
sweet chilli dressing place ingredients in screw-top jar; shake well.

on the table in 25 minutes
serves 4 **per serving** 6.1g total fat (0.7g saturated fat); 1354kJ (324 cal); 30.4g carbohydrate; 33g protein; 6.2g fibre
tips you will need to buy about 1kg of unpeeled prawns for this recipe. The dressing can be made two days ahead; assemble close to serving.

Hot-smoked trout and vermicelli salad

200g dried rice vermicelli noodles
400g hot-smoked trout fillets
2 trimmed celery stalks (200g), sliced thinly
2 lebanese cucumbers (300g), seeded, sliced thinly
½ cup (75g) toasted shelled pistachios
¼ cup coarsely chopped fresh mint
¼ cup coarsely chopped fresh thai basil
dressing
⅓ cup (80ml) lime juice
1 teaspoon chilli oil
1 tablespoon sesame oil
2 tablespoons fish sauce
1 clove garlic, crushed

1 Place noodles in large heatproof bowl of boiling water, stand until just tender; drain. Rinse under cold water; drain.
2 Meanwhile, make dressing.
3 Discard skin and bones from fish. Flake fish into large pieces in large bowl; add noodles, celery, cucumber, nuts and herbs.
4 Pour dressing over salad; toss gently to combine.
dressing place ingredients in screw-top jar; shake well.

on the table in 30 minutes
serves 4 **per serving** 21.1g total fat (3.1g saturated fat); 2031kJ (486 cal); 37.9g carbohydrate; 33.6g protein; 4.7g fibre
tips we used two hot-smoked ocean trout portions, weighing approximately 200g each, that were spiced with a blackening mixture of mountain pepper, native pepperberry, aniseed myrtle, salt and other flavourings before being "cooked" in hot smoking ovens. You can also use ordinary cold-smoked trout if hot-smoked trout is unavailable.

Tuna, olive and rocket pasta

250g angel hair pasta
425g can tuna chunks in olive oil, drained, flaked
⅓ cup (55g) seeded kalamata olives, quartered lengthways
250g cherry tomatoes, halved
⅓ cup (50g) toasted pine nuts
100g baby rocket leaves
dressing
2 tablespoons olive oil
1 tablespoon finely grated lemon rind
¼ cup (60ml) lemon juice
1 clove garlic, crushed
1 tablespoon dijon mustard

1 Cook pasta in large saucepan of boiling water, uncovered, until just tender; drain.
2 Meanwhile, make dressing.
3 Combine remaining ingredients in large bowl with pasta and dressing; toss gently to combine.
dressing place ingredients in screw-top jar; shake well.

on the table in 30 minutes
serves 4 **per serving** 30.8g total fat (3.9g saturated fat); 2521kJ (603 cal); 41.8g carbohydrate; 31g protein; 4.6g fibre
tips angel hair pasta, also known as capelli d'angelo, is a thin, narrow pasta that cooks very quickly. Do not overcook or it will become starchy and stodgy. This recipe is best made just before serving.

Calamari and vegetable salad

45g can anchovy fillets, drained
2 cloves garlic, crushed
¼ cup (60ml) olive oil
1 tablespoon chopped fresh flat-leaf parsley
400g frozen crumbed calamari rings
vegetable oil, for deep-frying
3 medium tomatoes (570g), quartered
1 tablespoon chopped fresh basil
1 medium green capsicum (200g), sliced thinly
1 medium avocado (250g), chopped coarsely
1 small green cucumber (130g), sliced thinly
½ cup (60g) seeded black olives
1 tablespoon white vinegar
4 large lettuce leaves, torn

1 Place anchovy in small bowl with half of the garlic, 1 tablespoon of the
olive oil and parsley. Let stand while preparing the salad.
2 Deep-fry calamari, in batches, in hot vegetable oil until golden brown;
drain on absorbent paper.
3 Place tomato, remaining garlic, basil, capsicum, avocado, cucumber
and olives in large bowl with combined remaining oil and vinegar;
toss to combine.
4 Place lettuce in serving bowl; top with salad, calamari and anchovy mixture.

on the table in 35 minutes
serves 4 **per serving** 47.1g total fat (7.7g saturated fat); 2541kJ
(608 cal); 20.1g carbohydrate; 24.1g protein; 6.1g fibre

Char-grilled tuna salad

600g tuna steak
2 medium red capsicums (400g), sliced thinly
200g mesclun
dressing
¼ cup (60ml) mirin
1 tablespoon light soy sauce
1 clove garlic, crushed
1 fresh small red thai chilli, chopped finely
1 green onion, chopped finely

1 Cook tuna on heated oiled grill plate (or grill or barbecue) until cooked as desired. Cover, rest 2 minutes; cut into thick slices.
2 Meanwhile, make dressing.
3 Combine tuna and dressing in large bowl with capsicum and mesclun; toss gently to combine.
dressing place ingredients in screw-top jar; shake well.

on the table in 15 minutes
serves 4 **per serving** 8.9g total fat (3.5g saturated fat); 1137kJ (272 cal); 4.6g carbohydrate; 40g protein; 2.2g fibre
tip brushing the whole piece of tuna with olive oil 3 hours ahead of cooking will help keep it moist and soft when it's grilled.

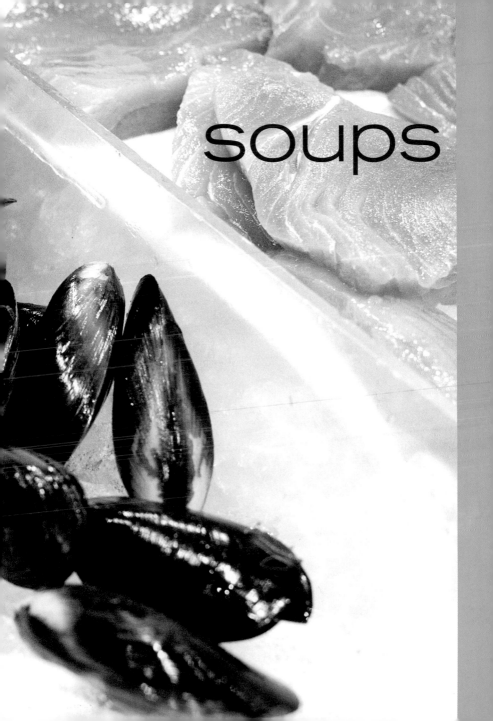

soups

Clam chowder

290g can baby clams
1 tablespoon olive oil
1 medium brown onion (150g), chopped finely
2 rashers rindless bacon (130g), chopped finely
2 tablespoons plain flour
½ cup (125ml) dry white wine
1½ cups (375ml) fish stock
2 cups (500ml) water
2 tablespoons tomato paste
1 teaspoon fresh thyme leaves
2 large potatoes (600g), chopped finely
300g white fish fillet, chopped coarsely
½ cup (60ml) cream
¼ cup coarsely chopped fresh parsley

1 Drain clams over a jug; reserve ¼ cup (60ml) of the liquid.
2 Heat oil in large saucepan; cook onion, stirring, until soft.
3 Add bacon; cook, stirring, 5 minutes. Add flour; cook, stirring, until
mixture thickens and bubbles. Gradually stir in wine, then stock, reserved
liquid, the water and tomato paste; cook, stirring, until mixture boils
and thickens.
4 Stir in thyme and potato; cook, covered, stirring occasionally, about
10 minutes or until the potato is almost tender.
5 Add fish; cook, covered, about 5 minutes or until just cooked. Stir in
clams, cream and parsley.

on the table in 35 minutes
serves 6 **per serving** 12.4g total fat (5.1g saturated fat); 1200kJ
(287 cal); 18.8g carbohydrate; 20.4g protein; 2.9g fibre

Tomato seafood soup

8 uncooked medium prawns (325g)
500g small black mussels
2 tablespoons extra virgin olive oil
2 cloves garlic, sliced thinly
½ teaspoon dried chilli flakes
2 medium potatoes (400g), chopped coarsely
½ cup (125ml) dry white wine
400g can chopped tomatoes
1½ cups (375ml) fish stock
½ cup (125ml) water
500g boneless white fish fillets, chopped coarsely
1 tablespoon lemon juice, approximately

1 Peel and devein prawns, leaving tails intact. Scrub mussels; remove beards.
2 Heat oil in large saucepan; cook garlic and chilli, stirring, until fragrant.
3 Add potato, wine, undrained tomatoes, stock and the water to pan; bring to a boil. Reduce heat, simmer, uncovered, about 10 minutes or until the potatoes are just tender.
4 Add fish, prawns and mussels; simmer, covered, until fish is cooked and mussels are open (discard any mussels that do not open). Stir in juice to taste.

on the table in 35 minutes
serve 4 **per serving** 13.8g total fat (2.9g saturated fat); 1647kJ (394 cal); 18.4g carbohydrate; 41.9g protein; 3.7g fibre
tip use a stiff brush to scrub the mussels under cold water.

Tom yum goong

16 uncooked medium king prawns (720g)
1 tablespoon peanut oil
10cm stick (20g) finely chopped fresh lemon grass
2 cloves garlic, crushed
4cm piece fresh ginger (20g), grated
3 cups (750ml) water
1.125 litres (4½ cups) fish stock
3 fresh small red thai chillies, sliced thinly
2 fresh kaffir lime leaves, shredded finely
¼ cup (60ml) fish sauce
⅓ cup (80ml) lime juice
4 green onions, sliced thinly
¼ cup loosely packed fresh coriander leaves
¼ cup loosely packed fresh thai basil leaves

1 Shell and devein prawns, leaving tails intact; reserve heads and shells.
2 Heat oil in large saucepan; cook prawn heads and shells, stirring, about 3 minutes or until they are deep orange in colour. Add lemon grass, garlic and ginger; cook, stirring, until fragrant.
3 Stir in the water, stock, chilli and lime leaves; bring to a boil. Reduce heat, simmer, uncovered, 10 minutes. Strain stock through muslin-lined sieve into large heatproof bowl; discard solids.
4 Return stock to same cleaned pan; bring to a boil. Add prawns, reduce heat; simmer, uncovered, until prawns are changed in colour. Remove from heat; stir in sauce and juice. Serve soup sprinkled with onion and herbs.

on the table in 35 minutes
serves 4 **per serving** 5.9g total fat (1g saturated fat); 686kJ (164 cal); 3.6g carbohydrate; 23.2g protein; 1.1g fibre

Prawn laksa

1kg medium uncooked prawns
1 tablespoon peanut oil
⅔ cup (200g) laksa paste
2 cloves garlic, crushed
1 teaspoon ground turmeric
2 x 400ml cans coconut milk
1 litre (4 cups) fish stock
2 kaffir lime leaves, sliced finely
250g egg noodles
4 green onions, sliced thinly
1 cup (80g) bean sprouts
¼ cup loosely packed fresh coriander leaves
1 tablespoon lime juice
2 teaspoons fish sauce

1 Shell and devein prawns, leaving tails intact.
2 Heat oil in large saucepan; cook paste, garlic and turmeric, stirring, until fragrant.
3 Add milk, stock and leaves; bring to a boil. Add noodles and prawns; simmer, uncovered, until prawns are just cooked. Add remaining ingredients; stir until hot.

on the table in 35 minutes
serves 6 **per serving** 32.7g total fat (25.1g saturated fat); 213kJ (519 cal); 28.4g carbohydrate; 26.2g protein; 3.9g fibre
tip if kaffir lime leaves are unavailable, use 2 teaspoons grated lime rind.

Cream of mussel soup

1kg small black mussels
1 cup (250ml) dry white wine
60g butter
8 green onions, chopped finely
½ teaspoon curry powder
¼ cup (35g) plain flour
1 cup (250ml) vegetable stock
2 cups (500ml) water
1 tablespoon tomato paste
¾ cup (180ml) cream
1 tablespoon finely chopped fresh dill

1 Scrub mussels; remove beards.
2 Place mussels and wine in large saucepan; cover, bring to a boil. Simmer about 5 minutes or until mussels open (discard any mussels that do not open). Drain mussels over medium heatproof bowl; reserve liquid.
3 Heat butter in large saucepan; cook onion and curry powder until onion is soft. Add flour; cook, stirring, about 2 minutes or until mixture thickens and bubbles. Gradually stir in reserved liquid, stock, the water and paste; stir until mixture boils and thickens.
4 Return mussels to pan with cream and dill; simmer, stirring, until heated through.

on the table in 35 minutes
serves 4 **per serving** 33.1g total fat (21.4g saturated fat); 1764kJ (422 cal); 12.2g carbohydrate; 9.2g protein; 1.1g fibre
tip use a stiff brush to scrub the mussels under cold water. Remove flour mixture from heat when adding liquid, to prevent lumps forming.

Spicy thai seafood soup

1 uncooked crab (325g)
200g white fish fillets
200g small black mussels
150g squid hoods
1.25 litres (5 cups) chicken stock
2 x 10cm sticks (40g) fresh lemon grass, chopped finely
4cm piece fresh galangal (20g), sliced thinly
4 fresh kaffir lime leaves
6 fresh small green thai chillies, chopped coarsely
4 dried long red thai chillies, chopped finely
8 uncooked large prawns (560g)
1 teaspoon grated palm sugar
2 tablespoons fish sauce
1 tablespoon lime juice
¼ cup loosely packed fresh thai basil leaves

1 Remove and discard back shell and gills of crab; rinse under cold water. Chop crab body into quarters, leaving claws intact. Cut fish into bite-sized portions. Scrub mussels; remove beards. Score inside of squid hoods in a diagonal pattern; cut into 2cm slices.
2 Place stock, lemon grass, galangal, lime leaves and the chillies in large saucepan; bring to a boil.
3 Add crab, fish, mussels, squid and unshelled prawns to boiling stock mixture; cook, uncovered, about 5 minutes or until seafood is just cooked through. Remove from heat (discard any mussels that do not open); stir in remaining ingredients. Serve hot.

on the table in 35 minutes
serves 4 **per serving** 3.7g total fat (1.3g saturated fat); 9.7kJ (217 cal); 5.9g carbohydrate; 39.2g protein; 0.9g fibre
tip use a stiff brush to scrub the mussels under cold water. The Thais sun-dry their chillies, but we can buy various types locally already dried: just be certain to buy sun- or oven-dried ones and not smoked, because the flavour is completely different. In Thai cooking, only the largest dried whole chillies are pulverised or ground for curry pastes or for addition to soups and stir-fries. They can be processed with or without the seeds, depending on how hot the dish is to be.

barbecues +grills

Barbecued chilli prawns with fresh mango salad

1kg uncooked large king prawns
½ teaspoon ground turmeric
1 teaspoon chilli powder
2 teaspoons sweet paprika
2 cloves garlic, crushed
mango salad
2 large mangoes (1.2kg), chopped coarsely
1 small red onion (100g), sliced thinly
1 fresh long red chilli, sliced thinly
1½ cups (120g) bean sprouts
½ cup coarsely chopped fresh coriander
2 teaspoons fish sauce
2 teaspoons grated palm sugar
2 tablespoons lime juice
1 tablespoon peanut oil

1 Make mango salad.
2 Shell and devein prawns, leaving tails intact.
3 Combine prawns, turmeric, chilli, paprika and garlic in large bowl.
4 Cook prawns, in batches, on heated oiled grill plate (or grill or barbecue) until prawns change in colour. Serve prawns with mango salad.
mango salad place ingredients medium bowl; toss gently to combine.

on the table in 35 minutes
serves 4 **per serving** 5.9g total fat (1g saturated fat); 1229kJ (294 cal); 30.3g carbohydrate; 29.5g protein; 5.1g fibre

Tuna skewers with soba

You need eight bamboo skewers for this recipe; soak them in cold water for at least an hour prior to use to prevent splintering or scorching.

800g tuna steaks, cut into 2cm pieces
2 tablespoons peanut oil
3 teaspoons wasabi paste
1 teaspoon ground coriander
⅓ cup finely chopped fresh coriander
300g dried soba noodles
1 medium carrot (120g), cut into matchsticks
4 green onions, sliced thickly
¼ cup firmly packed fresh coriander leaves
mirin dressing
¼ cup (60ml) mirin
2 tablespoons soy sauce
1cm piece fresh ginger (5g), grated
1 teaspoon sesame oil
1 teaspoon fish sauce
1 teaspoon caster sugar

1 Combine tuna, oil, wasabi and ground coriander in large bowl. Thread tuna onto eight skewers; sprinkle with chopped coriander.
2 Cook noodles in large saucepan of boiling water, uncovered, until just tender; drain. Rinse under cold water; drain.
3 Meanwhile, make mirin dressing.
4 Combine noodles in large bowl with carrot, onion, coriander leaves and half of the dressing.
5 Cook skewers on heated oiled grill plate (or grill or barbecue) until cooked as desired. Serve tuna skewers on noodles, drizzled with remaining dressing.
mirin dressing place ingredients in screw top jar; shake well.

on the table in 30 minutes
serves 4 **per serving** 22.5g total fat (6.2g saturated fat); 2847kJ (681 cal); 55g carbohydrate; 59.9g protein; 3.7g fibre

Thai fish burgers with sour and sweet green salad

500g boneless white fish fillets, chopped coarsely
1 tablespoon fish sauce
1 tablespoon kecap manis
1 clove garlic, quartered
1 fresh small red thai chilli, quartered
50g green beans, trimmed, chopped coarsely
¼ cup (15g) shredded coconut
¼ cup finely chopped fresh coriander
½ loaf turkish bread (215g)
⅓ cup (80ml) sweet chilli sauce
sour and sweet green salad
2 cups (120g) finely shredded iceberg lettuce
40g snow pea sprouts, chopped coarsely
1 telegraph cucumber (400g), seeded, sliced thinly
2 tablespoons lime juice
1 tablespoon fish sauce
1 tablespoon brown sugar

1 Blend or process fish, sauce, kecap manis, garlic and chilli until smooth. Place in large bowl with beans, coconut and coriander; using hand, combine ingredients then shape mixture into four patties.
2 Cook patties on heated oiled flat plate, covered, until cooked through.
3 Meanwhile, make sour and sweet green salad.
4 Cut bread in half; split halves horizontally. Toast, cut-side up. Divide bread among serving plates; top with salad, patties and chilli sauce.
sour and sweet green salad place ingredients in medium bowl; toss gently to combine.

on the table in 35 minutes
serves 4 **per serving** 8g total fat (3.4g saturated fat); 1639kJ (392 cal); 38.8g carbohydrate; 36.7g protein; 8.1g fibre
tip you need to buy a very small iceberg lettuce for this recipe.

Prawn, scallop and asparagus salad with ginger dressing

400g uncooked medium king prawns
400g scallops
250g asparagus, trimmed, halved
⅓ cup coarsely chopped fresh chives
120g baby spinach leaves
1 large red capsicum (350g), chopped coarsely
ginger dressing
5cm piece fresh ginger (25g), grated
1 tablespoon olive oil
2 tablespoons lemon juice
1 teaspoon white sugar

1 Shell and devein prawns, leaving tails intact
2 Cook prawns, scallops and asparagus, in batches, on heated oiled grill plate (or grill or barbecue) until cooked as desired.
3 Meanwhile, make ginger dressing.
4 Place prawns, scallops, asparagus, chives, spinach and capsicum in bowl with dressing; toss gently to combine.
ginger dressing press ginger between two spoons over large bowl to extract juice; discard fibres. Whisk in oil, juice and sugar until combined.

on the table in 35 minutes
serves 4 **per serving** 5.9g total fat (0.9g saturated fat); 765kJ (183 cal); 6.1g carbohydrate; 25g protein; 206g fibre

Mediterranean octopus salad with grilled tomatoes

4 large egg tomatoes (360g), halved
1 tablespoon fresh thyme leaves
2 tablespoons olive oil
1kg cleaned baby octopus
270g jar char-grilled red capsicum, drained, sliced thinly
1 medium oak leaf lettuce, torn
2 tablespoons drained capers, rinsed, chopped coarsely
2 lebanese cucumbers (260g), chopped coarsely
½ cup (75g) seeded kalamata olives, chopped coarsely
½ cup coarsely chopped fresh flat-leaf parsley
¼ cup (60ml) lemon juice
1 clove garlic, crushed

1 Place tomato, thyme and half of the oil in medium bowl; toss gently to combine. Cook on heated oiled flat plate, uncovered, until just softened and browned lightly.
2 Meanwhile, cook octopus, on heated oiled grill plate (or grill or barbecue) brushing with remaining oil, until just cooked through.
3 Combine remaining ingredients in large bowl with octopus; toss gently to combine. Serve salad with grilled tomato.

on the table in 20 minutes
serves 4 **per serving** 14.4g total fat (1.6g saturated fat); 1455kJ (348 cal); 9.7g carbohydrate; 43g protein; 3.1g fibre

Balmain bugs and citrus salad

2kg uncooked balmain bugs
1 tablespoon olive oil
2 teaspoons finely grated orange rind
2 tablespoons orange juice
1 tablespoon wholegrain mustard
citrus salad
1 medium grapefruit (425g)
1 large orange (300g)
1 lemon (140g)
150g curly endive, chopped coarsely
1 large fennel bulb (550g), trimmed, sliced thinly
1 tablespoon wholegrain mustard
1 tablespoon olive oil

1 Make citrus salad.
2 Place balmain bugs upside down on chopping board; cut tail from
body, discard body. Halve tail lengthways; discard back vein.
3 Cook bugs, on heated oiled grill plate (or grill or barbecue) until
cooked through.
4 Place bugs in large bowl with combined oil, rind, juice and mustard;
toss bugs to coat in mixture. Serve with citrus salad.
citrus salad cut unpeeled grapefruit, orange and lemon into equal size
wedges; cook on heated oiled grill plate, uncovered, until browned. Place
fruit in large bowl with endive, fennel and combined mustard and oil; toss
gently to combine.

on the table in 35 minutes
serves 4 **per serving** 11g total fat (1.6g saturated fat); 1258kJ (301 cal);
11.8g carbohydrate; 36g protein; 5.3g fibre
tip large king prawns or scampi are good substitutes for the bugs in
this recipe.

Grilled scallops with papaya salsa

800g firm payaya, chopped coarsely
2 medium tomatoes (380g), seeded, chopped coarsely
1 medium red onion (170g), chopped coarsely
¼ cup (60ml) lime juice
1 fresh small red thai chilli, chopped finely
2 tablespoons coarsely chopped fresh coriander
1 tablespoon vegetable oil
36 scallops with roe

1 Combine papaya, tomato, onion, juice, chilli, coriander and oil in large bowl.
2 Cook scallops, on heated oiled grill plate (or grill or barbecue) until browned both sides.
3 Serve papaya salsa topped with scallops.

on the table in 25 minutes
serves 4 **per serving** 6.4g total fat (1g saturated fat); 999kJ (239 cal); 15.2g carbohydrate; 27.3g protein; 5g fibre

Calamari teppanyaki

1½ cups (300g) white medium-grain rice
3 cups (750ml) water
1kg calamari rings
1 tablespoon peanut oil
1 fresh small red thai chilli, chopped finely
1 teaspoon finely grated lemon rind
1 clove garlic, crushed
2 tablespoons drained pickled pink ginger, sliced thinly
6 green onions, sliced thickly
2 lebanese cucumbers (260g), seeded, chopped finely
3 fresh small red thai chillies, chopped finely, extra
lemon soy dipping sauce
¼ cup (60ml) rice vinegar
1 tablespoon white sugar
1 tablespoon japanese soy sauce
1 teaspoon finely grated lemon rind

1 Make lemon soy dipping sauce.
2 Combine rice and the water in medium heavy-based saucepan, cover;
bring to a boil, stirring occasionally. Reduce heat, simmer, covered tightly,
about 10 minutes or until rice is cooked as desired. Remove from heat;
stand, covered, 5 minutes.
3 Meanwhile, combine calamari, oil, chilli, rind and garlic in large bowl.
4 Cook calamari mixture, on heated oiled flate plate (or grill or barbecue)
until tender.
5 Divide rice and calamari among serving plates with ginger, onion,
cucumber and extra chilli; serve with bowls of dipping sauce.
lemon soy dipping sauce heat vinegar, sugar and sauce in small
saucepan, stirring, until sugar dissolves. Remove from heat; stir in rind.

on the table in 30 minutes
serves 4 **per serving** 8.1g total fat (1.9g saturated fat); 2241kJ (536 cal);
65.9g carbohydrate; 47.6g protein; 2g fibre
tips teppanyaki is the name given to a traditional Japanese cooking style
where the food is cooked rapidly on a searingly hot grill plate on or near
the table. Pink pickled ginger, also known as gari, can be found in most
Asian grocery stores.

Salmon with garlic ginger butter

6 x 200g salmon fillets
150g butter, chopped
2 tablespoons soy sauce
2 cloves garlic, crushed
6cm piece fresh ginger (30g), grated
1 tablespoon brown sugar
1 teaspoon finely grated lemon rind
2 tablespoons lemon juice

1 Cook salmon on heated oiled grill plate (or grill or barbecue) until cooked as desired.
2 Meanwhile, stir remaining ingredients in small saucepan over low heat until butter melts.
3 Spoon butter mixture over salmon and serve with steamed rice and baby buk choy, if desired.

on the table in 20 minutes
serves 6 **per serving** 36.2g total fat (17g saturated fat); 2128kJ (509 cal); 3g carbohydrate; 43.6g protein; 0.3g fibre

Char-grilled lobster tail salad

4 uncooked small lobster tails in shell (800g)
2 radicchio (400g), trimmed, leaves separated
1 medium avocado (250g), chopped coarsely
4 radishes (140g), trimmed, sliced thinly
⅓ cup (50g) roasted pine nuts
4 green onions, sliced thinly
150g semi-dried tomatoes, drained, chopped coarsely
rosemary vinaigrette
⅓ cup (80ml) vegetable oil
¼ cup (60ml) red wine vinegar
1 tablespoon coarsely chopped fresh rosemary
1 tablespoon dijon mustard

1 Make rosemary vinaigrette.
2 Using kitchen scissors, discard soft shell from underneath lobster tails
to expose meat; cook, in batches, on heated oiled grill plate (or grill or
barbecue) until cooked through, brushing with a third of the vinaigrette.
Cut lobster tails in half lengthways.
3 Meanwhile, place remaining ingredients in large bowl with remaining
vinaigrette; toss gently to combine. Serve lobster on salad.
rosemary vinaigrette place ingredients in screw-top jar; shake well.

on the table in 35 minutes
serves 4 **per serving** 40.7g total fat (5.5g saturated fat); 2608kJ
(624 cal); 16.3g carbohydrate; 44.2g protein; 9.6g fibre

Spicy fish kebabs

1kg firm white fish fillets
1 tablespoon chopped fresh mint
1 tablespoon chopped fresh coriander
1 tablespoon chopped fresh flat-leaf parsley
2 fresh small red thai chillies, chopped finely
2 tablespoons lemon juice
1 tablespoon peanut oil
4 x 30cm-long lemon grass stems

1 Cut fish into 2cm pieces. Combine fish with herbs, chilli, juice and oil in medium bowl.
2 Cut lemon grass stems in half crossways; thread fish onto lemon grass skewers.
3 Cook fish on heated oiled grill plate (or grill or barbecue) until cooked as desired. Serve with lime wedges, if desired.

on the table in 30 minutes
serves 4 **per serving** 10.1g total fat (2.6g saturated fat); 1250kJ (299 cal); 0.4g carbohydrate; 51.2g protein; 0.2g fibre
tip we've used lemon grass stems as skewers in this recipe because they impart a fresh tangy flavour to the fish; you can use bamboo skewers, if you prefer. If using bamboo skewers, soak in water for a least 1 hour before use, to prevent them from scorching and splintering during cooking.

Chilli and garlic octopus

2 teaspoons coriander seeds, crushed
750g cleaned baby octopus
2 tablespoons olive oil
2 cloves garlic, crushed
1 tablespoon lemon juice
2 tablespoons sweet chilli sauce
2 cups (40g) trimmed watercress

1 Heat small dry frying pan, add coriander; cook, stirring, until fragrant. Remove from heat.
2 Combine octopus and coriander in large bowl with oil, garlic, juice and sauce.
3 Cook octopus, on heated oiled grill plate (or grill or barbecue) until just cooked through. Serve octopus tossed with watercress.

on the table in 20 minutes
serves 4 **per serving** 12.8g total fat (2.1g saturated fat); 1371kJ (328 cal); 4.2g carbohydrate; 48.1g protein; 1.1g fibre
tip if you are unable to find cleaned baby octopus, buy 1kg of whole baby octopus; remove and discard heads and beaks from all then cut each octopus in half.

Prawn and green onion skewers

You need 12 bamboo skewers for this recipe; soak them in cold water for at least an hour prior to use to prevent splintering or scorching. If using metal skewers, oil them first to stop the prawns from sticking.

36 uncooked medium king prawns (1.6kg)
2 tablespoons lime juice
1 tablespoon olive oil
2 cloves garlic, crushed
12 green onions
2 limes, cut into wedges

1 Shell and devein prawns, leaving tails intact.
2 Combine prawns, juice, oil and garlic in medium bowl.
3 Cut onions into 4cm lengths. Thread prawns and onion onto skewers.
4 Cook skewers, on heated oiled grill plate (or grill or barbecue) until prawns change in colour. Serve with lime wedges.

on the table in 35 minutes
serves 4 **per serving** 5.9g total fat (0.9g saturated fat); 974kJ (233 cal); 2g carbohydrate; 41.9g protein; 1.4g fibre

Mussels with beer

1kg large black mussels
1 tablespoon olive oil
2 cloves garlic, crushed
1 large red onion (300g), sliced thinly
2 fresh long red chillies, sliced thinly
1½ cups (375ml) beer
2 tablespoons sweet chilli sauce
1 cup coarsely chopped fresh flat-leaf parsley
garlic bread
1 large turkish bread (430g)
50g butter, melted
2 cloves garlic, crushed
2 tablespoons finely chopped fresh flat-leaf parsley

1 Scrub mussels; remove beards
2 Make garlic bread.
3 Meanwhile, heat oil on heated flat plate; cook garlic, onion and chilli, stirring, until onion softens. Add mussels and combined beer and chilli sauce; cook, covered, about 5 minutes or until mussels open (discard any that do not open). Remove from heat; stir in parsley.
4 Serve mussels with garlic bread.
garlic bread halve bread horizontally; cut each half into four pieces, brush with combined butter, garlic and parsley. Cook bread on heated oiled grill plate, uncovered, until browned both sides.

on the table in 35 minutes
serves 4 **per serving** 19.7g total fat (8.3g saturated fat); 2169kJ (519 cal); 58.7g carbohydrate; 17.5g protein; 5.6g fibre
tip use a stiff brush to scrub the mussels under cold water.

Fish with coriander pesto

4 x 200g white fish steaks
coriander pesto
½ cup firmly packed fresh coriander leaves
2 tablespoons peanut oil
1 tablespoon salted roasted peanuts
1 fresh small red thai chilli, chopped finely
2 tablespoons lime juice

1 Make coriander pesto.
2 Brush fish with half of the coriander pesto; reserve remaining pesto.
3 Cook fish on heated oiled grill plate (or grill or barbecue) until cooked as desired.
4 Serve fish brushed with reserved pesto and, if desired, a mixed green salad with snow pea sprouts.
coriander pesto blend or process ingredients until well combined.

on the table 20 minutes
serves 4 **per serving** 14.8g total fat (3.2g saturated fat); 1271kJ (304 cal); 0.4g carbohydrate; 41.7g protein; 0.6g fibre

Salmon steaks with tarragon sauce and grilled asparagus

800g potatoes, sliced thickly
500g asparagus, trimmed
4 x 200g salmon fillets
tarragon sauce
20g butter
1 medium brown onion (150g), chopped finely
½ cup (125ml) dry white wine
300ml cream
2 tablespoons finely chopped fresh tarragon

1 Make tarragon sauce.
2 Meanwhile, boil, steam or microwave potato until just tender; drain.
3 Cook potato, asparagus and fish on heated oiled grill plate, (or grill or barbecue) until potato is browned, asparagus just tender and fish is cooked as desired.
4 Serve fish with potato, asparagus and sauce.

tarragon sauce melt butter in small saucepan; cook onion, stirring, until soft. Add wine; bring to a boil. Reduce heat, simmer, uncovered, until liquid reduces by half. Add cream; simmer, uncovered, about 10 minutes or until sauce thickens slightly. Remove from heat; stir in tarragon.

on the table in 35 minutes
serves 4 **per serving** 51g total fat (27.3g saturated fat); 3361kJ (804 cal); 31.7g carbohydrate; 48g protein; 5g fibre

Crisp-skinned snapper with stir-fried vegetables and black beans

½ teaspoon sea salt
1 teaspoon coarsely ground black pepper
4 x 200g snapper fillets
1 teaspoon sesame oil
1 large brown onion (200g), cut into thin wedges
1 clove garlic, crushed
1cm piece fresh ginger (5g), grated
1 tablespoon salted black beans, rinsed, drained
1 medium green capsicum (200g), chopped coarsely
1 medium red capsicum (200g), chopped coarsely
6 green onions, sliced thickly
100g snow peas
100g broccolini, chopped coarsely
½ cup (125ml) water
¼ cup (60ml) oyster sauce
2 tablespoons lemon juice
500g baby buk choy, chopped coarsely
1 cup (80g) bean sprouts

1 Combine salt and pepper in small bowl; rub into skin side of each fillet. Cook fish, skin-side down, on heated oiled grill plate (or grill or barbecue) until browned and crisp; turn, cook until browned and cooked as desired. Cover to keep warm.
2 Heat oil in wok; stir-fry brown onion, garlic and ginger until onion softens. Add beans; stir-fry 1 minute. Add capsicums, green onion, snow peas and broccolini; stir-fry until vegetables are just tender.
3 Stir in the water, sauce and juice; cook, stirring, until mixture thickens slightly. Add buk choy and bean sprouts; stir-fry until heated through. Serve fish on vegetables.

on the table in 25 minutes
serves 4 **per serving** 5.3g total fat (1.4g saturated fat); 1296kJ (310 cal); 14.2g carbohydrate; 47.6g protein; 6.1g fibre

Grilled tuna with red cabbage salad

1 tablespoon olive oil
1 medium red onion (170g), sliced thinly
2 cups (160g) finely shredded red cabbage
2 cups (160g) finely shredded wombok
¼ cup (60ml) cider vinegar
1 large green apple (200g), sliced thinly
1 cup loosely packed fresh flat-leaf parsley leaves
4 x 200g tuna steaks

1 Heat oil in wok; stir-fry onion and cabbages about 2 minutes. Add vinegar; bring to a boil. Boil 1 minute. Remove from heat; stir in apple and parsley.
2 Meanwhile, cook tuna on heated oiled grill plate (or grill or barbecue) until cooked as desired.
3 Serve fish with warm cabbage salad.

on the table in 25 minutes
serves 4 **per serving** 16.2g total fat (5.2g saturated fat); 1685kJ (403 cal); 8.9g carbohydrate; 52.7g protein; 5.1g fibre

Char-grilled salmon with avocado salsa

4 x 200g salmon fillets
2 small avocados (400g), sliced thinly
1 small red onion (100g), sliced thinly
2 tablespoons chopped fresh dill
2 tablespoons drained baby capers
100g baby rocket leaves
lemon dressing
2 tablespoons lemon juice
⅓ cup (80ml) olive oil

1 Make lemon dressing.
2 Cook salmon on heated oiled grill plate (or grill or barbecue) until cooked as desired.
3 Meanwhile, combine avocado, onion, dill and capers in medium bowl.
4 Serve salmon with rocket and avocado salsa; drizzle with dressing.
lemon dressing place ingredients in screw-top jar with salt and pepper to taste; shake well.

on the table in 25 minutes
serves 4 **per serving** 48.5g total fat (9.2 saturated fat); 2558kJ (612 cal); 3.1g carbohydrate; 41.4g protein; 1.9g fibre

Fish with tahini dressing and eggplant salad

2 large eggplants (1kg), sliced thickly
6 boneless white fish fillets (1.2kg)
3 medium tomatoes (450g), seeded, sliced thickly
1 medium red capsicum (200g), sliced thickly
½ cup firmly packed fresh flat-leaf parsley leaves
¼ cup firmly packed fresh oregano leaves
2 tablespoons olive oil
¼ cup (60ml) lemon juice
2 tablespoons toasted pine nuts
tahini dressing
1 cup (280g) greek-style yogurt
½ cup (125ml) tahini
1 clove garlic, crushed
½ cup (50g) walnuts, chopped coarsely
1 small red onion (100g), chopped coarsely
1 fresh small red thai chilli, chopped coarsely
2 tablespoons lemon juice
¼ cup finely chopped fresh coriander

1 Cook eggplant on heated oiled grill plate (or grill or barbecue),
until tender.
2 Meanwhile, make tahini dressing.
3 Cook fish on heated oiled grill plate (or grill or barbecue) until cooked
as desired.
4 Place eggplant in large bowl with remaining ingredients; toss gently
to combine.
5 Serve fish with salad, dressing and lemon wedges, if desired.
tahini dressing blend or process yogurt, tahini, garlic, nuts, onion, chilli
and juice until smooth; stir in coriander.

on the table in 30 minutes
serves 6 **per serving** 36.3g total fat (6.6g saturated fat); 2537kJ
(607 cal); 13.4g carbohydrate; 53.1g protein; 9.3g fibre

Char-grilled tuna with chilled soba

4 x 200g tuna steaks
2 tablespoons mirin
1 tablespoon tamarind concentrate
400g dried soba noodles
2 tablespoons toasted sesame seeds
4 green onions, sliced thinly lengthways
dressing
¼ cup (60ml) tamari
1 teaspoon wasabi paste
2 teaspoons sesame oil
2 tablespoons lime juice

1 Combine fish, mirin and tamarind in medium bowl.
2 Meanwhile, cook noodles in large saucepan of boiling water, uncovered, until just tender; drain. Rinse under cold water; drain.
3 Cook tuna on heated oiled grill plate (or grill or barbecue) until cooked as desired.
4 Make dressing.
5 Place noodles and dressing in medium bowl with seeds and all but 1 tablespoon of the onion; toss gently to combine.
6 Divide noodles among serving plates; top with tuna, sprinkle with remaining onion.
dressing place ingredients in screw-top jar; shake well.

on the table in 35 minutes
serves 4 **per serving** 18g total fat (5.5g saturated fat); 2989kJ (715 cal); 69.9g carbohydrate; 63.7g protein; 4.2g fibre
tips wasabi is Japanese horseradish sold in powdered or paste form. Soba are Japanese buckwheat noodles and are great served hot or cold.

Prawns with pistachio potato salad

1kg uncooked large king prawns
2 teaspoons ground cumin
2 teaspoons ground coriander
1 teaspoon hot paprika
1 clove garlic, crushed
1 lime, quartered
pistachio potato salad
700g tiny new potatoes, halved
1 cup (150g) toasted shelled pistachios, chopped coarsely
¼ cup (60ml) lime juice
2 tablespoons olive oil
4 green onions, sliced thinly
1 medium red onion (170g), chopped finely

1 Shell and devein prawns, leaving tails intact.
2 Combine prawns, cumin, coriander, paprika and garlic in medium bowl.
3 Make pistachio potato salad.
4 Meanwhile, cook prawns, in batches, on heated oiled grill plate (or grill or barbecue) until prawns change in colour. Add lime to grill plate; cook until heated through.
5 Serve prawns and lime with potato salad.
pistachio potato salad boil, steam or microwave potatoes until tender, drain. Place potatoes in large bowl with remaining ingredients; toss gently to combine.

on the table in 30 minutes
serves 4 **per serving** 28g total fat (3.4g saturated fat); 2295kJ (549 cal); 31.8g carbohydrate; 38.6g protein; 7.8g fibre

Fish with grilled corn salad

4 x 200g boneless white fish fillets
2 tablespoons soy sauce
grilled corn salad
2 corn cobs (500g), silk and husks removed
250g cherry tomatoes, halved
1 small red onion (100g), sliced thinly
1 fresh small red thai chilli, sliced thinly
2 medium avocados (500g), chopped coarsely
¼ cup coarsely chopped fresh coriander
⅓ cup (80ml) lime juice
1 clove garlic, crushed
1 tablespoon olive oil

1 Make grilled corn salad.
2 Brush fish with sauce; cook fish on heated oiled grill plate (or grill or
barbecue) until cooked as desired.
3 Serve fish with corn salad.
grilled corn salad cook corn on heated oiled grill plate (or grill or
barbecue) until browned and just tender; cool 10 minutes. Using
sharp knife, remove kernels from cob; combine in medium bowl with
remaining ingredients.

on the table in 35 minutes
serves 4 **per serving** 30g total fat (5.2g saturated fat); 2077kJ (497 cal);
18.7g carbohydrate; 41.9g protein; 6.9g fibre

Fish with thai dressing

4 x 200g white fish steaks
thai dressing
⅓ cup (80ml) sweet chilli sauce
½ cup (125ml) lime juice
1 tablespoon fish sauce
2 teaspoons finely chopped fresh lemon grass
2 tablespoons finely chopped fresh coriander
½ cup finely chopped fresh mint
1cm piece fresh ginger (5g), grated

1 Make thai dressing.
2 Cook fish on heated oiled grill plate (or grill or barbecue) until cooked as desired.
3 Serve fish drizzled with dressing and, if desired, with a mixed salad and lemon wedges.
thai dressing place ingredients in screw-top jar; shake well.

on the table in 15 minutes
serves 4 **per serving** 5.1g total fat (1.5g saturated fat); 995kJ (238 cal); 5g carbohydrate; 41.9g protein; 1.6g fibre
tip we used swordfish, but you can use tuna steaks or cutlets.

Grilled tuna with egg salad

¼ cup (75g) mayonnaise
2 teaspoons drained baby capers
1 tablespoon finely chopped drained cornichons
1 tablespoon lemon juice
4 x 200g tuna steaks
2 tablespoons olive oil
4 hard-boiled eggs, quartered
fresh watercress sprigs

1 Combine mayonnaise in small bowl with capers, cornichons and juice.
2 Brush tuna with oil; cook on heated oiled grill plate (or grill or barbecue) until cooked as desired.
3 Serve tuna topped with egg, mayonnaise mixture and watercress.

on the table in 30 minutes
serves 4 **per serving** 31.9g total fat (8.2g saturated fat); 2253kJ (53 cal); 6g carbohydrate; 57.2g protein; 0.4g fibre

Moroccan fish kebabs with almond and lemon couscous

You need eight 25cm bamboo skewers for this recipe; soak them in cold water for at least an hour prior to use to prevent splintering or scorching.

½ cup finely chopped fresh coriander
2 cloves garlic, crushed
2 tablespoons olive oil
2 fresh small red thai chillies, chopped finely
¼ cup (60ml) lemon juice
800g firm white fish fillets, cut into 3cm pieces
1½ cups (375ml) chicken stock
1½ cups (300g) couscous
½ cup firmly packed fresh coriander leaves
1 tablespoon finely chopped preserved lemon
¼ cup (35g) toasted slivered almonds

1 Combine chopped coriander, garlic, oil, chilli and juice in small bowl.
2 Combine fish and half of the coriander mixture in large bowl; thread fish onto skewers.
3 Bring stock to a boil in small saucepan; remove from heat. Add couscous to stock, cover; stand about 5 minutes or until liquid is absorbed, fluffing with fork occasionally. Add remaining coriander mixture, coriander leaves, lemon and nuts; toss gently to combine.
4 Meanwhile, cook kebabs on heated oiled grill plate (or grill or barbecue) until cooked as desired. Serve with couscous.

on the table in 35 minutes
serves 4 **per serving** 16g total fat (2.2g saturated fat); 2391kJ (572 cal); 59.2g carbohydrate; 46.6 protein; 2.6g fibre
tips use the softened, salty rind of preserved lemon to add a tangy intensity to this dish.

Salmon with mango and pineapple salsa

4 x 200g salmon cutlets
mango and pineapple salsa
2 small mangoes (600g), chopped coarsely
1 small pineapple (800g), chopped coarsely
2 tablespoons coarsely chopped fresh mint
2 tablespoons coarsely chopped fresh coriander
2 fresh small red thai chillies, sliced thinly
2 green onions, sliced thinly
2 tablespoons lime juice
1 tablespoon light olive oil

1 Make mango and pineapple salsa.
2 Cook salmon on heated oiled grill plate (or grill or barbecue) until cooked as desired. Serve salmon with salsa.
mango and pineapple salsa place ingredients in medium bowl; toss gently to combine.

on the table in 20 minutes
serves 4 **per serving** 16.3g total fat (3.2g saturated fat); 1584kJ (379 cal); 22.3g carbohydrate; 33.6g protein; 4.1g fibre

Grilled snapper fillets with fennel and onion salad

4 x 200g snapper fillets
1 medium red onion (170g), sliced thinly
4 green onions, sliced thinly
1 large fennel bulb (550g), trimmed, sliced thinly
2 trimmed celery stalks (200g), sliced thinly
½ cup coarsely chopped fresh flat-leaf parsley
dressing
⅓ cup (80ml) orange juice
¼ cup (60ml) olive oil
2 cloves garlic, crushed
2 teaspoons sambal oelek

1 Make dressing.
2 Cook fish on heated oiled grill plate (or grill or barbecue) until cooked as desired.
3 Combine onions, fennel, celery and parsley in medium bowl with half of the dressing; toss gently to combine.
4 Serve salad topped with fish; drizzle with remaining dressing.
dressing place ingredients in screw-top jar; shake well.

on the table in 25 minutes
serves 4 **per serving** 18.3g total fat (3.3g saturated fat); 1580kJ (378 cal); 8g carbohydrate; 43g protein; 4.5g fibre

Asian-flavoured ocean trout with shiitake mushrooms

1 tablespoon salted black beans, rinsed, drained
1 clove garlic, crushed
3cm piece fresh ginger (15g), grated
1 teaspoon dried chilli flakes
⅓ cup (80ml) soy sauce
6 green onions, sliced thinly
4 whole rainbow trout (2kg)
400g fresh shiitake mushrooms
2 tablespoons lemon juice

1 Crush beans in small bowl. Add garlic, ginger, chilli, half of the soy sauce and half of the onion; stir to combine.
2 Place each fish on oiled piece of foil large enough to completely enclose it; place a quarter of the bean mixture inside each fish, wrap tightly in foil. Cook fish on heated oiled grill plate (or grill or barbecue) until cooked as desired.
3 Meanwhile, cook mushrooms on heated oiled flat plate, uncovered, until tender; drizzle with remaining soy sauce.
4 Serve mushrooms with fish, drizzled with juice and sprinkled with remaining onion.

on the table in 25 minutes
serves 4 **per serving** 10.5g total fat (2.5g saturated fat); 1430kJ (342 cal); 5.1g carbohydrate; 54.6g protein; 2.9g fibre

Cajun fish with lime

4 x 250g fish cutlets
2 teaspoons ground cumin
2 teaspoons ground coriander
2 teaspoons sweet paprika
2 teaspoons mustard powder
2 teaspoons onion powder
½ teaspoon garlic powder
¼ teaspoon cayenne pepper
2 teaspoons fennel seeds
2 limes, sliced thickly

1 Combine fish with spices, powders, pepper and seeds in large bowl.
2 Cook fish on heated oiled grill plate (or grill or barbecue) until cooked as desired.
3 Meanwhile, cook lime on heated oiled grill plate until browned both sides.
4 Divide fish among serving plates; top with lime slices.

on the table in 15 minutes
serves 4 **per serving** 4.5g total fat (1.4g saturated fat); 869kJ (208 cal); 0.3g carbohydrate; 41g protein; 0.5g fibre

Fish with spinach and skordalia

Skordalia is a tangy Greek sauce or dip made with pureed cooked potato, and breadcrumbs or ground nuts. Skordalia can be served with almost any kind of dish – from grilled meats and poultry to fish and raw vegetables.

2 medium potatoes (400g), chopped coarsely
3 cloves garlic, crushed
2 slices stale white bread
⅓ cup (80ml) olive oil
1 tablespoon lemon juice
1 tablespoon white wine vinegar
⅓ cup (95g) yogurt
1 teaspoon finely chopped fresh mint
2 teaspoons lemon juice, extra
4 x 200g white fish steaks
2 teaspoons olive oil, extra
400g baby spinach leaves

1 Boil, steam or microwave potato until tender; drain. Mash potato in large bowl with garlic.
2 Meanwhile, trim and discard crusts from bread. Soak bread in small bowl of cold water; drain. Squeeze out excess water. Add bread to potato mixture; beat with electric mixer until smooth. Gradually beat in combined oil, juice and vinegar until smooth.
3 Combine yogurt, mint and extra juice in small bowl.
4 Cook fish on heated oiled grill plate (or grill or barbecue) until cooked as desired; cover to keep warm.
5 Meanwhile, heat extra oil in large saucepan; cook spinach, stirring, until just wilted.
6 Divide skordalia among serving plates; top with fish, spinach and yogurt mixture.

on the table in 35 minutes
serves 4 **per serving** 5.6g total fat (1g saturated fat); 468kJ (112 cal); 4.6g carbohydrate; 10.2g protein; 1.2g fibre
tip white wine vinegar is a pale, slightly pungent vinegar made from fermented white wine, and can be found at your local supermarket.

Char-grilled chilli squid salad

1kg whole baby squid
¼ cup (60ml) olive oil
2 teaspoons sea salt flakes
4 medium red chillies, chopped finely
2 cloves garlic, chopped finely
2 tablespoons finely chopped fresh oregano
350g baby egg truss tomatoes
½ cup firmly packed fresh mint leaves
¼ cup firmly packed fresh flat-leaf parsley leaves
100g baby spinach
1 tablespoon lemon juice
1 tablespoon extra virgin olive oil, extra

1 Gently pull head and entrails away from the squid, then remove the clear quill (backbone) and discard. Cut tentacles from head just below eyes of squid; remove beak from the centre of the tentacles. Pull away membrane from squid hood and flaps (wings); wash hood, tentacles and flaps.
2 Place a palette knife or wooden spatula inside a squid tube (this prevents cutting all the way through). Using a large knife, slice the squid along its length at 1cm intervals, giving a concertina effect. Repeat with remaining squid.
3 Combine squid tubes, tentacles and flaps, oil, salt, chilli, garlic, and oregano in medium bowl.
4 Cook squid, on heated oiled grill plate (or grill or barbecue) until just cooked through.
5 Arrange halved tomatoes, mint, parsley, spinach and squid on plates. Drizzle with combined juice and extra oil.

on the table in 35 minutes
serves 4 **per serving** 19.8g total fat (3g saturated fat); 1129kJ (270 cal); 2.4g carbohydrate; 19.8g protein; 2.6g fibre

Grilled fish with tamarind stir-fried vegetables

2 teaspoons peanut oil
5cm piece fresh ginger (25g), cut into matchstick-sized pieces
2 cloves garlic, crushed
2 fresh long red chillies, chopped finely
1 medium red capsicum (200g), sliced thinly
¼ cup (60ml) chicken stock
2 tablespoons oyster sauce
1 tablespoon fish sauce
2 tablespoons grated palm sugar
1 tablespoon tamarind concentrate
250g baby buk choy, chopped coarsely
280g gai lan, chopped coarsely
8 green onions, cut into 3cm lengths
½ cup firmly packed fresh coriander leaves
4 x 200g white fish steaks

1 Heat oil in wok; stir-fry ginger, garlic and chilli until fragrant. Add capsicum; stir-fry until capsicum is tender. Add stock, sauces, sugar and tamarind; bring to a boil. Boil 1 minute. Add buk choy, gai larn and onion; stir-fry until greens are just wilted. Remove from heat; stir in coriander.
2 Meanwhile, cook fish on heated oiled grill plate (or grill or barbecue) until cooked as desired.
3 Serve fish with vegetables.

on the table in 30 minutes
serves 4 **per serving** 7.3g total fat (1.9g saturated fat); 1296kJ (310 cal); 14.2g carbohydrate; 44.6g protein; 3.4g fibre

Fish with thai salad

100g snow pea sprouts, trimmed
1 cup loosely packed fresh mint leaves
½ cup loosely packed fresh coriander leaves
3 shallots (75g), sliced thinly
2 fresh long red chillies, sliced thinly
4 x 200g white fish fillets
⅓ cup (80ml) lime juice
2 tablespoons grated palm sugar
1 tablespoon fish sauce

1 Combine sprouts, mint, coriander, shallots and chilli in medium bowl.
2 Cook fish on heated oiled grill plate (or grill or barbecue) until cooked as desired.
3 Meanwhile, combine juice, sugar and sauce in small bowl.
4 Serve fish with salad drizzled with dressing.

on the table in 25 minutes
serves 4 **per serving** 1.6g total fat (0.3g saturated fat); 907kJ (217 cal); 13g carbohydrate; 36.8g protein; 2.6g fibre

Garlic prawn, capsicum and artichoke salad

1kg uncooked large king prawns
4 cloves garlic, crushed
1 fresh small red thai chilli, chopped finely
2 tablespoons olive oil
500g small jerusalem artichokes
1 medium red capsicum (200g)
100g baby rocket leaves
caper dressing
¼ cup (60ml) lemon juice
2 tablespoons olive oil
1 tablespoon drained capers, rinsed, chopped finely
1 teaspoon dijon mustard

1 Shell and devein prawns, leaving tails intact. Combine prawns with garlic, chilli and half of the oil in large bowl.
2 Make caper dressing.
3 Scrub artichokes under water; halve lengthways. Toss artichokes with remaining oil in medium bowl; cook on heated grill plate (or grill or barbecue) until tender.
4 Meanwhile, quarter capsicum; discard seeds and membranes. Cook capsicum, uncovered, on heated oiled grill plate (or grill or barbecue) until tender; slice thickly.
5 Cook prawns, in batches, on heated oiled grill plate (or grill or barbecue) until prawns change in colour.
6 Place prawns, artichokes and capsicum in large bowl with rocket and dressing; toss gently to combine.
caper dressing place ingredients in screw-top jar; shake well.

on the table in 35 minutes
serves 4 **per serving** 19.4g total fat (2.7g saturated fat); 1342kJ (321 cal); 5.8g carbohydrate; 29.1g protein; 3.7g fibre

Char-grilled baby octopus salad

750g cleaned baby octopus
1 clove garlic, crushed
1cm piece fresh ginger (5g), grated
2 teaspoons dry sherry
1 teaspoon brown sugar
1 teaspoon malt vinegar
½ teaspoon sesame oil
2 teaspoons kecap manis
2 teaspoons sweet chilli sauce
¼ cup (60ml) tomato sauce
250g cherry tomatoes, halved
1 small red onion (100g), sliced thinly
150g mesclun
2 lebanese cucumbers (260g), seeded, sliced thinly
⅓ cup coarsely chopped fresh coriander
dressing
¼ cup (60ml) sweet chilli sauce
1 tablespoon light soy sauce
1 clove garlic, crushed
1 tablespoon lime juice

1 Combine octopus with garlic, ginger, sherry, sugar, vinegar, oil, kecap manis and sauces in large bowl.
2 Make dressing.
3 Cook octopus, on heated oiled grill plate (or grill or barbecue) until just cooked through.
4 Place octopus in large bowl with tomato, onion, mesclun, cucumber, coriander and dressing; toss gently to combine.
dressing combine ingredients in glass screw-top jar; shake well.

on the table in 30 minutes
serves 4 **per serving** 2.7g total fat (0.2g saturated fat); 936kJ (224 cal); 13.6g carbohydrate; 33.1g protein; 4.2g fibre
tip if you are unable to find cleaned baby octopus, buy 1kg of whole baby octopus; remove and discard heads and beaks from all then cut each octopus in half.

Whiting in vine leaves

16 pickled vine leaves
16 whiting fillets (1.2 kg)
freshly ground black pepper
¼ cup (60ml) extra virgin olive oil
2 medium eggplants (600g), sliced
8 green banana chillies
8 yellow banana chillies

1 Rinse vine leaves, drain and pat dry. Sprinkle fish with pepper. Wrap the centre of each fish fillet in a vine leaf, leaving the ends open. Brush fish on both sides with some of the oil.
2 Brush eggplant with remaining oil. Cook eggplant and chillies on a heated oiled grill plate (or grill or barbecue); cover to keep warm.
3 Cook fish on heated oiled grill plate (or grill or barbecue) until cooked as desired. Serve fish with grilled vegetables.

on the table in 35 minutes
serves 8 **per serving** 8.5g total fat (1.3g saturated fat); 1007kJ (241 cal); 6.3g carbohydrate; 32.4g protein; 4.9g fibre

pan-fries+
stir-fries

Mussel broth with black bean sauce

1 cup (200g) jasmine rice
1kg small black mussels
1 cup (250ml) water
⅓ cup (80ml) black bean sauce
2 large fresh red chillies, sliced thinly
4 green onions, sliced thinly

1 Add rice to large saucepan of boiling water. Boil, uncovered, until just
tender; drain. Cover to keep warm.
2 Meanwhile, scrub mussels; remove beards.
3 Place the water, black bean sauce and chilli in large saucepan;
bring to a boil.
4 Add mussels; cook, covered, about 3 minutes or until mussels open
(discard any that do not). Sprinkle with green onions.
5 Serve rice in bowls, topped with mussels and broth.

on the table in 35 minutes
serves 4 **per serving** 0.9g total fat (0.2g saturated fat); 527kJ (126 cal);
23.4g carbohydrate; 5.2g protein; 0.6g fibre
tip use a stiff brush to scrub the mussels under cold water.

Chilli crab

4 small crabs (1.5kg)
1 tablespoon peanut oil
2 fresh small red thai chillies, chopped finely
4cm piece fresh ginger (20g), grated
2 cloves garlic, crushed
2 teaspoons fish sauce
1 tablespoon brown sugar
¼ cup (60ml) lime juice
¼ cup (60ml) rice vinegar
¼ cup (60ml) fish stock
3 green onions, sliced thickly
¼ cup firmly packed fresh coriander leaves

1 Holding crab firmly, slide a sharp, strong knife under top of shell at back, lever off shell. Remove and discard whitish gills. Rinse well under cold water. Cut crab body in quarters with cleaver or strong sharp knife.
2 Heat oil in wok; cook chilli, ginger, garlic, sauce, sugar, juice, vinegar and stock, stirring, until sugar has dissolved.
3 Add crab; cook, covered, about 15 minutes or until crab has changed in colour. Stir in onion and coriander.

on the table in 35 minutes
serves 4 **per serving** 5.8g total fat (1g saturated fat); 727kJ (174 cal); 6.8g carbohydrate; 23.1g protein; 0.9g fibre
tip use shell crackers (like nut crackers) to make eating the crab easier.

Stir-fried octopus with thai basil

1kg baby octopus
2 teaspoons peanut oil
2 teaspoons sesame oil
2 cloves garlic, crushed
2 fresh small red thai chillies, sliced thinly
2 large red capsicums (700g), sliced thinly
6 green onions, cut into 2cm lengths
¼ cup firmly packed thai basil leaves
¼ cup (60ml) fish sauce
¼ cup (65g) grated palm sugar
1 tablespoon kecap manis

1 Remove and discard head and beak of each octopus; cut each octopus in half. Rinse under cold water; drain.
2 Heat peanut oil in wok; stir-fry octopus, in batches, until browned all over and tender. Cover to keep warm.
3 Heat sesame oil in wok; stir-fry garlic, chilli and capsicum until capsicum is just tender. Return octopus to wok with remaining ingredients; stir-fry until basil leaves wilt and sugar dissolves.

on the table in 30 minutes
serves 4 **per serving** 6.7g total fat (0.7g saturated fat); 1442kJ (345 cal); 23.7g carbohydrate; 45.3g protein; 2.6g fibre

Fettuccine with creamy salmon and dill sauce

375g fettuccine pasta
½ cup (120g) light sour cream
2 tablespoons lemon juice
415g can red salmon, drained
1 small red onion (100g), sliced thinly
¼ cup loosely packed fresh dill
2 tablespoons drained small capers
1 tablespoon grated lemon rind

1 Cook pasta in large saucepan of boiling water, uncovered, until tender; drain.
2 Meanwhile, combine sour cream and juice in small bowl. Break the salmon into chunks.
3 Toss hot pasta with sour cream mixture, salmon, onion, dill and capers until combined. Serve topped with lemon rind.

on the table in 20 minutes
serves 4 **per serving** 17.5g total fat (7g saturated fat); 2391kJ (572 cal); 69.5g carbohydrate; 32g protein; 3g fibre

Prawn tamarind stir-fry with buk choy

1kg uncooked medium king prawns
2 tablespoons peanut oil
4 green onions, sliced thinly lengthways
4 cloves garlic, sliced thinly
1 teaspoon cornflour
½ cup (125ml) vegetable stock
2 tablespoons oyster sauce
1 tablespoon tamarind concentrate
1 teaspoon sambal oelek
2 teaspoons sesame oil
1 tablespoon lime juice
1 tablespoon brown sugar
350g yellow patty-pan squash, sliced thickly
300g sugar snap peas, trimmed
800g baby buk choy, chopped coarsely

1 Shell and devein prawns, leaving tails intact.
2 Heat half of the peanut oil in wok; stir-fry onion and garlic, separately, until browned lightly. Drain on absorbent paper.
3 Blend cornflour and stock in small jug; stir in sauce, tamarind, sambal, sesame oil, juice and sugar.
4 Heat remaining peanut oil in wok; stir-fry prawns, in batches, until changed in colour and almost cooked through.
5 Stir-fry squash in wok until just tender. Add cornflour mixture; stir-fry until sauce boils and thickens slightly. Return prawns to wok with peas and buk choy; stir-fry until buk choy just wilts and prawns are cooked through.
6 Serve stir-fry with steamed jasmine rice and topped with reserved onion and garlic.

on the table in 35 minutes
serves 4 **per serving** 13.3g total fat (2.2g saturated fat); 1392kJ (333 cal); 16.2g carbohydrate; 33.5g protein; 7.2g fibre

Crisp-skinned ocean trout with bavette

375g bavette pasta
¼ cup (60ml) vegetable oil
¼ cup loosely packed fresh sage leaves
¼ cup (50g) drained capers, rinsed
6 green onions, cut into 5cm lengths
4 x 200g ocean trout fillets, skin-on
⅓ cup (80ml) lemon juice
1 tablespoon sweet chilli sauce
2 cloves garlic, crushed

1 Cook pasta in large saucepan of boiling water, uncovered, until just tender.
2 Meanwhile, heat oil in large frying pan; shallow-fry sage, capers and onion, separately, until crisp.
3 Cook fish, skin-side up, on heated oiled grill pan until crisp both sides and cooked as desired.
4 Meanwhile, place drained pasta in large bowl with juice, chilli sauce, garlic and half of the sage, half of the capers and half of the onion; toss gently to combine.
5 Divide pasta mixture among serving plates; top with fish, sprinkle with remaining sage, remaining capers and remaining onion.

on the table in 30 minutes
serves 4 **per serving** 22.7g total fat (3.8g saturated fat); 2863kJ (685 cal); 67.3g carbohydrate; 49.9g protein; 4.1g fibre

American crab cakes

2 x 170g cans crab meat, drained
1 egg, beaten lightly
6 green onions, sliced thinly
2 tablespoons mayonnaise
1 tablespoon dijon mustard
1 cup (70g) fresh breadcrumbs
1 tablespoon worcestershire sauce
1 tablespoon chopped fresh flat-leaf parsley
¼ teaspoon sweet paprika
¼ cup (25g) packaged breadcrumbs
¼ cup (60ml) vegetable oil

1 Combine crab, egg, onion, mayonnaise, mustard, fresh breadcrumbs, sauce, parsley and paprika in medium bowl. Shape mixture into four patties; coat in packaged breadcrumbs.
2 Heat oil in medium frying pan; cook patties until browned both sides and cooked through.

on the table in 30 minutes
makes 4 **per crab cake** 19.7g total fat (2.7g saturated fat); 1333kJ (319 cal); 20.6g carbohydrate; 14.2g protein; 1.6g fibre
tip the crab cakes will hold together a little better if you have time to refrigerate the patties for 1 hour prior to cooking.

Sumac, salt and pepper fish with mediterranean salad

1 cup (200g) couscous
1 cup (250ml) boiling water
1 tablespoon olive oil
2 tablespoons sumac
1 teaspoon salt
1 teaspoon cracked black pepper
4 x 200g firm white fish fillets
1 lemon, quartered
mediterranean salad
2 medium tomatoes (300g), seeded, chopped coarsely
2 medium red capsicums (400g), chopped coarsely
2 tablespoons seeded kalamata olives, chopped coarsely
2 tablespoons drained baby capers, rinsed
1 cup coarsely chopped fresh flat-leaf parsley

1 Combine couscous and the water in large heatproof bowl. Cover; stand about 5 minutes or until water is absorbed, fluffing with fork occasionally. Stir in oil.
2 Make mediterranean salad.
3 Combine sumac, salt and pepper in large bowl, add fish; turn fish to coat in mixture. Cook fish, in batches, in heated oiled large frying pan until cooked as desired.
4 Divide couscous among plates, top with salad and fish; serve with lemon.
mediterranean salad place ingredients in medium bowl; toss gently to combine.

on the table in 30 minutes
serves 4 **per serving** 9.7g total fat (2.1g saturated fat); 1990kJ (476 cal); 45.7g carbohydrate; 49.9g protein; 3.9g fibre

Thai prawns with garlic

1kg uncooked medium king prawns
2 teaspoons coarsely chopped fresh coriander root and stem mixture
2 teaspoons dried coriander seeds
1 teaspoon dried green peppercorns
4 cloves garlic, quartered
2 tablespoons peanut oil
1 cup (80g) bean sprouts
1 tablespoon finely chopped fresh coriander
1 tablespoon fried shallot
1 tablespoon fried garlic
1 tablespoon fresh coriander leaves

1 Shell and devein prawns, leaving tails intact.
2 Using mortar and pestle, crush coriander root and stem mixture, coriander seeds, peppercorns and garlic to a paste.
3 Combine prawns and coriander paste in large bowl with half of the oil. Cover; refrigerate 10 minutes.
4 Heat remaining oil in wok; stir-fry prawn mixture, in batches, until prawns are changed in colour. Remove from heat; stir sprouts and chopped coriander through stir-fry. Serve sprinkled with fried shallot, fried garlic and coriander leaves.

on the table in 35 minutes
serves 4 **per serving** 10.2g total fat (1.8g saturated fat); 849kJ (203 cal); 0.8g carbohydrate; 26.5g protein; 1.2g fibre
tip fried shallot (homm jiew) and fried garlic (kratiem jiew) are used as condiments on the table or sprinkled over cooked dishes. Both can be purchased canned or in cellophane bags at Asian grocery stores; once opened, leftovers will keep for months if tightly sealed. Make your own by slicing shallots or garlic thinly and shallow-frying in vegetable oil until golden-brown and crisp.

Fish cutlets with pesto butter

80g butter, softened
2 tablespoons prepared basil pesto
¼ teaspoon cracked black pepper
1 teaspoon finely grated lemon rind
4 x 200g white fish cutlets
100g baby spinach leaves, trimmed

1 Blend or process butter, pesto, pepper and rind in small bowl until well combined.
2 Cook fish, in batches, in large heated oiled frying pan until browned both sides and cooked as desired.
3 Place butter mixture in same pan; stir over low heat until butter melts. Return fish to pan; coat with melted butter mixture.
4 Serve fish with baby spinach leaves.

on the table in 20 minutes
serves 4 **per serving** 24.9g total fat (13.4g saturated fat); 1526kJ (365 cal); 0.4g carbohydrate; 35g protein; 1g fibre
tip there are many versions of basil pesto you can buy – some are sold fresh, under refrigeration, while others are available bottled on supermarket shelves. Experiment until you find one you like best.

Prawn, asparagus and sesame stir-fry

1kg uncooked large king prawns
2 teaspoons sesame seeds
1 tablespoon peanut oil
1cm piece fresh ginger (5g), grated
2 cloves garlic, crushed
1 medium brown onion (150g), sliced thinly
300g asparagus, trimmed, chopped
1 fresh large red chilli, sliced thinly
2 tablespoons rice wine
¼ cup (60ml) soy sauce
2 teaspoons sesame oil
2 teaspoons brown sugar

1 Shell and devein prawns, leaving tails intact.
2 Cook sesame seeds in dry, heated wok, stirring, until browned lightly and fragrant. Remove from wok.
3 Heat half of the peanut oil in wok; stir-fry ginger, garlic and onion until fragrant. Add asparagus; stir-fry until just tender. Remove from wok.
4 Heat remaining oil in wok; stir-fry prawns, in batches, until just changed in colour. Return asparagus mixture and all prawns to wok with chilli and combined remaining ingredients; stir-fry until hot. Serve sprinkled with sesame seeds.

on the table in 30 minutes
serves 4 **per serving** 10g total fat (1.6g saturated fat); 991kJ (237 cal); 5.4g carbohydrate; 28.3g protein; 1.6g fibre

Fish in spicy coconut cream

2 teaspoons peanut oil
2 cloves garlic, crushed
1cm piece fresh ginger (5g), grated finely
20g piece fresh turmeric, grated finely
2 fresh small red thai chillies, sliced thinly
1½ cups (375ml) fish stock
400ml can coconut cream
4cm piece fresh galangal (20g), halved
10cm stick (20g) fresh lemon grass, cut into 2cm pieces
4 x 200g white fish fillets
2 tablespoons fish sauce
2 green onions, sliced thinly

1 Heat oil in wok; stir-fry garlic, ginger, turmeric and chilli until fragrant.
Add stock, coconut cream, galangal and lemon grass; bring to a boil.
Add fish; reduce heat, simmer, covered, until fish is cooked as desired.
2 Using slotted spoon, remove fish carefully from liquid; place in serving
bowl, cover to keep warm.
3 Remove and discard galangal and lemon grass pieces from liquid.
Bring sauce to a boil; boil 5 minutes. Remove from heat; stir in sauce
and onion. Pour liquid over fish in bowl.

on the table in 35 minutes
serves 4 **per serving** 27.7g total fat (0.8g saturated fat); 915kJ (219 cal);
26.3g carbohydrate; 15.3g protein; 11.2g fibre

Prawn green curry

1kg uncooked medium king prawns
2 cups (400g) jasmine rice
1 tablespoon peanut oil
1 small brown onion (80g), sliced thinly
1cm piece fresh ginger (5g), grated
2 fresh kaffir lime leaves, sliced thinly
¼ cup (75g) green curry paste
1⅔ cups (410ml) coconut milk
½ cup (125ml) water
1 tablespoon fish sauce
1 tablespoon lime juice
1 tablespoon brown sugar
100g snake beans, cut into 4cm lengths
¼ cup firmly packed thai basil leaves

1 Shell and devein prawns, leaving tails intact.
2 Cook rice in large saucepan of boiling water, uncovered, until just tender; drain. Cover to keep warm.
3 Meanwhile, heat oil in wok; cook onion, ginger, lime leaves and paste, stirring, until onion softens. Stir in coconut milk and the water; bring to a boil. Reduce heat, simmer, uncovered, 5 minutes.
4 Add prawns to wok with sauce, juice, sugar and beans; simmer, stirring, about 5 minutes or until prawns are changed in colour and just cooked through. Remove from heat; stir in basil. Serve curry with rice.

on the table in 30 minutes
serves 4 **per serving** 33g total fat (20.3g saturated fat); 3407kJ (815 cal); 89.4g carbohydrate; 36.8g protein; 5.6g fibre
tip substitute red curry paste for green curry paste if you prefer.

Poached salmon with dill yogurt sauce

2kg whole salmon or ocean trout
2 sprigs fresh dill
2 sprigs fresh flat-leaf parsley
¼ teaspoon whole black peppercorns
1 cup (250ml) dry white wine
dill yogurt sauce
500g greek-style yogurt
2 shallots (50g), chopped finely
1 tablespoon finely chopped fresh dill

1 Wipe fish dry with absorbent paper. Place fish, herbs, peppercorns
and wine in fish poacher. Add enough water to completely cover fish.
Bring slowly to a simmer. The liquid must not boil.
2 Poach fish about 12 minutes or until cooked as desired.
3 When fish is cooked, lift tray with fish on it from the poaching liquid.
Allow to drain well. Discard liquid and herbs. Transfer fish to serving
platter; remove skin from the top of fish.
4 Meanwhile, make dill yogurt sauce.
5 Serve salmon with sauce.
dill yogurt sauce combine ingredients in medium bowl.

on the table in 35 minutes
serves 10 **per serving** 11g total fat (4g saturated fat); 953kJ (228 cal);
4.7g carbohydrate; 23.5g protein; 0.1g fibre

Chilli squid fettuccine

500g fettuccine pasta
½ cup (125ml) olive oil
450g small squid hoods, sliced thinly
2 fresh long red chillies, sliced thinly
2 cloves garlic, crushed
250g rocket leaves, torn
100g fetta cheese, crumbled

1 Cook pasta in large saucepan of boiling water, uncovered, until just tender; drain.
2 Meanwhile, heat 1 tablespoon of the oil in large shallow frying pan; cook squid, in batches, over high heat, until tender and browned lightly.
3 Add remaining oil to pan with chilli and garlic; cook, stirring, until fragrant. Add rocket; cook, stirring, until just wilted.
4 Place pasta in large bowl with squid, rocket mixture and cheese; toss gently to combine.

on the table in 20 minutes
serves 6 **per serving** 25g total fat (5.7g saturated fat); 2378kJ (569 cal); 59.7g carbohydrate; 26g protein; 5g fibre

Mussels with basil and lemon grass

1kg black mussels
1 tablespoon peanut oil
1 medium brown onion (150g), chopped finely
2 cloves garlic, crushed
10cm stick (20g) fresh lemon grass, chopped finely
1 fresh small red thai chilli, chopped finely
1 cup (250ml) dry white wine
2 tablespoons lime juice
2 tablespoons fish sauce
½ cup loosely packed thai basil leaves
½ cup (125ml) coconut milk
1 fresh small red thai chilli, sliced thinly
2 green onions, sliced thinly

1 Scrub mussels; remove beards
2 Heat oil in wok; stir-fry brown onion, garlic, lemon grass and chopped chilli until onion softens and mixture is fragrant
3 Add wine, juice and sauce to wok; bring to a boil. Add mussels; reduce heat, simmer, covered, about 5 minutes or until mussels open (discard any that do not).
4 Meanwhile, shred half of the basil finely. Add shredded basil and coconut milk to wok; stir-fry until heated through. Place mussel mixture in serving bowl; sprinkle with sliced chilli, green onion and remaining basil.

on the table in 30 minutes
serves 4 **per serving** 12.1g total fat (6.8g saturated fat); 886kJ (212 cal); 6.9g carbohydrate; 8.4g protein; 1.7g fibre
tip use a stiff brush to scrub the mussels under cold water.

Salt and pepper scallops with cherry tomato salsa

1kg scallops
2 teaspoons sea salt
½ teaspoon cracked black pepper
2 cloves garlic, crushed
1 tablespoon peanut oil
cherry tomato salsa
400g cherry tomatoes, quartered
2 lebanese cucumbers (260g), seeded, chopped finely
1 medium red onion (170g), chopped finely
4 green onions, sliced thinly
2 tablespoons lemon juice
2 fresh small red thai chillies, chopped finely

1 Combine scallops with salt, pepper and garlic in medium bowl; use fingers to sprinkle salt mixture evenly over each scallop. Cover; refrigerate 15 minutes.
2 Meanwhile, make cherry tomato salsa.
3 Heat oil in wok; stir-fry scallops, in batches, until salt-pepper coating is browned and scallops are cooked as desired.
4 Add scallops to salsa; toss gently to combine.
cherry tomato salsa combine ingredients in large bowl.

on the table in 35 minutes
serves 4 **per serving** 6.6g total fat (1.3g saturated fat); 924kJ (221 cal); 7.9g carbohydrate; 30.7g protein; 3.2g fibre

Mustard-seed chilli prawns

1kg uncooked large king prawns
¼ teaspoon ground turmeric
2 fresh small red thai chillies, chopped finely
2 tablespoons vegetable oil
2 teaspoons black mustard seeds
2 cloves garlic, crushed
2 green onions, sliced thinly
2 tablespoons finely chopped fresh coriander

1 Shell and devein prawns, leaving tails intact. Cut along back of prawn, taking care not to cut all the way through; flatten prawn slightly.
2 Rub turmeric and chilli into prawns in medium bowl.
3 Heat oil in large frying pan; cook mustard seeds and garlic, stirring, until seeds start to pop. Add prawn mixture; cook, stirring, until prawns just change colour. Stir in onion and coriander.

on the table in 30 minutes
serves 4 **per serving** 10g total fat (1.3g saturated fat); 815kJ (195 cal); 0.2g carbohydrate; 25.8g protein; 0.3g fibre
tip mustard seeds are available in black, brown or yellow varieties; here, we used black, as they are more spicy and piquant than the other varieties. You can purchase mustard seeds from major supermarkets or health food shops.

Fish with herb and tomato dressing

12 baby new potatoes (480g), halved
4 medium green zucchini (480g), quartered
2 tablespoons olive oil
4 x 200g white fish fillets
2 medium egg tomatoes (150g), chopped finely
2 tablespoons lemon juice
1 tablespoon finely chopped fresh dill
2 tablespoons finely chopped fresh basil

1 Boil, steam or microwave potato and zucchini, separately, until tender; drain.
2 Meanwhile, heat half of the oil in large frying pan; cook fish until cooked as desired. Remove from pan; cover to keep warm.
3 Heat remaining oil in same cleaned pan; cook tomato and juice, stirring, 2 minutes. Remove from heat; stir in herbs.
4 Divide fish and vegetables among serving plates; drizzle with tomato mixture.

on the table in 30 minutes
serves 4 **per serving** 10.8g total fat (1.5g saturated fat); 1371kJ (328 cal); 18.5g carbohydrate; 38.1g protein; 4.6g fibre

Prawn, lime and rice noodle stir-fry

650g uncooked large king prawns
375g thick rice stick noodles
1 tablespoon sesame oil
2 cloves garlic, crushed
2cm piece fresh ginger (10g), grated
2 fresh small red thai chillies, sliced thinly
250g broccolini, quartered
⅓ cup (80ml) lime juice
¼ cup (60ml) light soy sauce
2 teaspoons fish sauce
4 green onions, sliced thinly
2 tablespoons coarsely chopped fresh mint

1 Shell and devein prawns, leaving tails intact.
2 Place noodles in large heatproof bowl, cover with boiling water; stand until just tender, drain.
3 Meanwhile, heat oil in wok; stir fry garlic, ginger and chilli until fragrant. Add broccolini; stir-fry until just tender. Add prawns; stir-fry until just changed in colour. Add noodles and remaining ingredients; stir-fry until hot.

on the table in 30 minutes
serves 4 **per serving** 6.5g total fat (0.7g saturated fat); 1789kJ (428 cal); 62.2g carbohydrate; 26.7g protein; 4.8g fibre
tip broccolini, sweeter than broccoli with a subtle peppery edge, is completely edible, from flower to stem. Substitute gai lan or broccoli if broccolini is not available.

Combination chow mein

400g uncooked medium king prawns
2 tablespoons peanut oil
250g chicken mince
100g chinese barbecued pork, sliced thinly
1 medium carrot (120g), sliced thinly
1 medium brown onion (150g), sliced thinly
2 trimmed celery stalks (200g), sliced thinly
1 medium green capsicum (200g), sliced thinly
100g button mushrooms, sliced thinly
2 cups (140g) coarsely shredded wombok
1 cup (80g) bean sprouts
3 green onions, sliced thinly
2 teaspoons cornflour
2 tablespoons light soy sauce
2 tablespoons oyster sauce
½ cup (125ml) chicken stock
2 x 100g packets fried noodles

1 Shell and devein prawns, leaving tails intact.
2 Heat half of the oil in wok; stir-fry prawns until just changed in colour. Remove prawns from wok; cover to keep warm.
3 Add chicken to wok; stir-fry until cooked through. Add pork; stir-fry until heated through. Remove from wok; cover to keep warm.
4 Heat remaining oil in wok; stir-fry carrot and brown onion until onion softens. Add celery, capsicum and mushrooms; stir-fry until vegetables are just tender.
5 Return prawns and chicken mixture to wok with wombok, sprouts, green onion and blended cornflour, sauces and stock; stir-fry until wombok just wilts and sauce boils and thickens. Serve on noodles.

on the table in 30 minutes
serves 4 **per serving** 23.2g total fat (6.7g saturated fat); 1848kJ (442 cal); 21.1g carbohydrate; 34.1g protein; 6.5g fibre
tips although chow mein is traditionally made with egg noodles, you can use any noodles you like – we used packaged crunchy fried noodles. Chinese barbecued pork has a sweet-sticky coating made from soy sauce, sherry, five-spice and hoisin sauce, and is traditionally cooked in special ovens. It is available from Asian barbecue shops. You will also need about half a small wombok for this recipe.

Fish with wasabi mayonnaise

2 cups (400g) white long-grain rice
1 tablespoon peanut oil
4 x 200g white fish fillets
500g gai lan
wasabi mayonnaise
⅓ cup (100g) mayonnaise
2 teaspoons wasabi paste
2 green onions, chopped finely
2 tablespoons coarsely chopped fresh coriander
2 tablespoons lime juice

1 Make wasabi mayonnaise.
2 Cook rice in large saucepan of boiling water, uncovered, until just tender; drain.
3 Meanwhile, heat oil in large frying pan; cook fish, in batches, until browned both sides and cooked as desired. Cover to keep warm.
4 Boil, steam or microwave gai lan until just tender; drain.
5 Divide gai lan among serving plates; top with fish and mayonnaise. Serve with rice.
wasabi mayonnaise combine ingredients in small bowl; cover.

on the table in 15 minutes
serves 4 **per serving** 17.8g total fat (3.2g saturated fat); 2968kJ (710 cal); 85.6g carbohydrate; 49.2g protein; 2.7g fibre
tip for a stronger, more fiery taste, add an extra teaspoon of wasabi to the mayonnaise mixture.

Seafood combination omelette

12 eggs, beaten lightly
4 green onions, sliced thinly
1 tablespoon vegetable oil
1 clove garlic, crushed
1 fresh small red thai chilli, sliced thinly
650g scallops, halved
400g small shelled cooked prawns
400g cooked crab meat
2 tablespoons light soy sauce
⅓ cup firmly packed fresh coriander
2 tablespoons coarsely chopped fresh mint

1 Whisk egg and onion together in large bowl.
2 Brush medium heated frying pan with a little of the oil. Add a quarter of the egg mixture; swirl to cover base of pan. Cook, covered, 3 minutes or until cooked through. Remove omelette; repeat with remaining egg mixture to make three more omelettes.
3 Meanwhile, heat remaining oil in wok; stir-fry garlic, chilli and scallops until scallops are cooked through.
4 Add prawns, crab, sauce and herbs; stir until heated through.
5 Divide seafood mixture among omelettes; roll to enclose filling.
Cut each omelette in half diagonally.

on the table in 25 minutes
serves 4 **per serving** 22.5g total fat (5.9g saturated fat); 1960kJ (469 cal); 3.7g carbohydrate; 62.7g protein; 0.7g fibre
tip we removed the roe from the scallops, but it can be left intact, if you prefer.

Hokkien noodles with prawns

1.2 kg uncooked large king prawns
500g hokkien noodles
300g baby buk choy, quartered lengthways
2 teaspoons peanut oil
1 fresh small red thai chilli, chopped finely
1 clove garlic, crushed
¼ cup (60ml) water
2 tablespoons sesame oil
½ cup (125ml) kecap manis
¼ cup (60ml) light soy sauce
½ cup coarsely chopped fresh coriander

1 Shell and devein prawns, leaving tails intact.
2 Place noodles in large heatproof bowl; cover with boiling water. Use fork to separate noodles; drain. Rinse again by pouring boiling water over noodles in colander, drain.
3 Heat half of the peanut oil in wok; stir-fry chilli and garlic briefly, until just fragrant. Add prawns, in batches; stir-fry over high heat until just changed in colour.
4 Heat remaining peanut oil in wok; stir-fry noodles and buk choy over high heat until buk choy just wilts.
5 Return prawns to wok with the water, sesame oil, kecap manis, sauce and coriander; stir-fry briefly over high heat until prawn mixture is just hot.

on the table in 30 minutes
serves 4 **per serving** 13.9g total fat (2.1g saturated fat); 2249kJ (538 cal); 66.7g carbohydrate; 45.8g protein; 3.6g fibre
tips you can use any fresh Asian noodle you like in this recipe – hokkien, stir-fry or rice – but check the manufacturer's instructions regarding the required length of time they are to be soaked (or cooked) in hot water before using because they all differ.

Mixed seafood with crisp thai basil

250g squid hoods
250g white fish fillets
600g uncooked medium king prawns
250g baby octopus
2 tablespoons peanut oil
1 clove garlic, crushed
2 fresh small red thai chillies, sliced thinly
1 medium carrot (120g), halved, sliced thinly
1 medium red capsicum (200g), sliced thinly
4 green onions, sliced thinly
1 tablespoon fish sauce
1 teaspoon oyster sauce
1 tablespoon lime juice
¼ cup (60ml) peanut oil, extra
⅓ cup loosely packed thai basil leaves

1 Score squid in a diagonal pattern. Cut squid and fish into 3cm pieces; shell and devein prawns, leaving tails intact. Remove and discard head and beak of each octopus; cut each octopus in half. Rinse under cold water; drain.
2 Heat half of the oil in wok; stir-fry seafood, in batches, until prawns are changed in colour, fish is cooked as desired, and squid and octopus are tender. Cover to keep warm.
3 Heat remaining oil in wok; stir-fry garlic, chilli and carrot until carrot is just tender. Add capsicum; stir-fry until capsicum is just tender. Return seafood to wok with onion, sauces and juice; stir-fry until hot.
4 Heat extra oil in small frying pan until sizzling; fry basil leaves, in batches, until crisp but still green. Drain on absorbent paper. Top seafood with basil leaves.

on the table in 35 minutes
serves 4 **per serving** 26g total fat (4.9g saturated fat); 1906kJ (456 cal); 4.4g carbohydrate; 50.5g protein; 1.8g fibre

Bavette with prawns, peas, lemon and dill

1kg uncooked large king prawns
375g bavette pasta
2 tablespoons olive oil
2 cloves garlic, crushed
1½ cups (180g) frozen peas
2 teaspoons finely grated lemon rind
6 green onions, sliced thinly
1 tablespoon coarsely chopped fresh dill
¼ cup (60ml) lemon juice

1 Shell and devein prawns; halve lengthways.
2 Cook pasta in large saucepan of boiling water, uncovered, until just tender; drain. Return to pan.
3 Meanwhile, heat half of the oil in large frying pan; cook garlic and prawns, in batches, until prawns are just changed in colour. Cover to keep warm.
4 Cook peas in same frying pan, stirring, until heated through. Add rind, onion and dill; cook, stirring, until onion is just tender. Return prawns to frying pan with juice; stir until heated through.
5 Add prawn mixture and remaining oil to hot pasta; toss gently to combine.

on the table in 30 minutes
serves 4 **per serving** 15.7g total fat (2.3g saturated fat); 2441kJ (584 cal); 69.8g carbohydrate; 39.2g protein; 8g fibre

Salmon in sesame crust

2 cups (400g) medium-grain white rice
2 tablespoons sesame seeds
1 teaspoon coriander seeds
1 teaspoon black peppercorns
4 x 200g skinless salmon fillets
1 tablespoon vegetable oil
1 tablespoon sesame oil
1 clove garlic, crushed
1cm piece fresh ginger (5g), grated
1 fresh small red thai chilli, sliced thinly lengthways
500g baby buk choy, quartered lengthways
¼ cup (60ml) salt-reduced soy sauce
1 tablespoon mirin
2 tablespoons honey
2 tablespoons lime juice

1 Cook rice in large saucepan of boiling water, uncovered, until just tender; drain. Cover to keep warm.
2 Meanwhile, place seeds and peppercorns in strong plastic bag; crush with rolling pin or meat mallet. Coat one side of each fish fillet with seed mixture.
3 Heat vegetable oil in large frying pan; cook fish, seeded-side down, for 1 minute. Turn; cook until fish is cooked as desired.
4 Meanwhile, heat sesame oil in wok; stir-fry garlic, ginger and chilli until fragrant. Add remaining ingredients; stir-fry until buk choy just wilts.
5 Serve fish with rice and buk choy.

on the table in 20 minutes
serves 4 **per serving** 27.3g total fat (4.9g saturated fat); 3457kJ (827 cal); 92.8g carbohydrate; 49.1g protein; 3.2g fibre

Sweet and spicy mussels with stir-fried asian greens

1kg black mussels
1 tablespoon peanut oil
1 clove garlic, crushed
8cm piece fresh ginger (40g), chopped finely
⅓ cup (80ml) pure maple syrup
2 tablespoons soy sauce
1 tablespoon oyster sauce
¼ cup (60ml) fish stock
1 tablespoon lemon juice
4 green onions, sliced thinly
300g baby buk choy, chopped coarsely
400g gai lan, chopped coarsely
2 cups (160g) bean sprouts

1 Scrub mussels; remove beards.
2 Heat oil in wok; stir-fry garlic and ginger until fragrant. Add syrup, sauces, stock and juice; bring to a boil. Add mussels; return to a boil. Reduce heat; simmer, covered, about 5 minutes or until mussels open (discard any that do not). Remove mussels; cover to keep warm.
3 Return stock mixture to a boil. Add remaining ingredients to wok; stir-fry until greens are just wilted.
4 Return mussels to wok; stir-fry until heated through. Accompany with steamed jasmine rice, if desired.

on the table in 35 minutes
serves 4 **per serving** 6g total fat (1.1g saturated fat); 840kJ (201 cal); 24.7g carbohydrate; 10g protein; 3.8g fibre
tip use a stiff brush to scrub the mussels under cold water.

Easy paella

1 tablespoon olive oil
100g chorizo sausage, sliced thinly
1 medium brown onion (150g), sliced thinly
2 cloves garlic, crushed
1 medium red capsicum (200g), sliced thinly
2 cups (400g) medium-grain white rice
¼ teaspoon ground turmeric
1 cup (250ml) water
1 cup (250ml) fish stock
400g can tomatoes, drained, chopped coarsely
1 cup (125g) frozen peas
500g seafood marinara mix
300g white fish fillets, chopped coarsely

1 Heat oil in large frying pan; cook chorizo, onion and garlic, stirring, until onion softens. Add capsicum, rice and turmeric; cook, stirring, 1 minute. Stir in the water, stock and tomato; bring to a boil. Reduce heat, simmer, covered, 5 minutes.
2 Place peas, marinara mix and fish on rice in frying pan; cook, covered, over low heat about 10 minutes or until rice is tender and seafood is cooked through.

on the table in 30 minutes
serves 4 **per serving** 8.7g total fat (5.4g saturated fat); 3248kJ (777 cal); 87.5g carbohydrate; 61.3g protein; 4.2g fibre

Seared ocean trout with buk choy

1 litre (4 cups) water
¼ cup (60ml) soy sauce
1 star anise
1 teaspoon sambal oelek
1 tablespoon honey
800g baby buk choy, halved lengthways
1 tablespoon sesame oil
4 x 220g ocean trout fillets

1 Combine the water, sauce, star anise, sambal and honey in medium saucepan; bring to a boil. Cook buk choy in boiling stock until just wilted. Remove buk choy; cover to keep warm. Strain stock into medium bowl; discard solids.
2 Return stock to heat; boil, uncovered, while cooking fish.
3 Heat oil in large frying pan; sear fish over high heat until cooked as desired. Serve fish on buk choy; drizzle with hot stock.

on the table in 25 minutes
serves 4 **per serving** 13.4g total fat (2.6g saturated fat); 1438kJ (344 cal); 8.4g carbohydrate; 45.6g protein; 2.6g fibre

Fish with celery and bean salad

4 x 200g white fish steaks
dressing
⅓ cup (80ml) lemon juice
2 cloves garlic, chopped finely
¼ teaspoon salt
¼ teaspoon cracked black pepper
⅓ cup (80ml) olive oil
1 tablespoon fresh oregano leaves, torn
1 tablespoon baby capers rinsed, drained
celery and bean salad
2 trimmed celery stalks (200g), halved, sliced thinly
300g can cannellini beans, rinsed, drained
¼ cup coarsely chopped young celery leaves

1 Make dressing.
2 Make celery and bean salad, add ¼ cup (60ml) of the dressing; toss gently to combine.
3 Heat oiled, large frying pan; cook fish until browned on both sides and cooked as desired. Remove from pan.
4 Add remaining dressing to same pan; bring to a boil.
5 Serve salad topped with fish, drizzled with warm dressing.
dressing combine juice, garlic, salt, pepper and oil in small bowl; whisk until thickened slightly. Stir in oregano and capers.
celery and bean salad combine ingredients in small bowl.

on the table in 20 minutes
serves 4 **per serving** 23.1g total fat (4g saturated fat); 1768kJ (423 cal); 7.1g carbohydrate; 44.6g protein; 4.7g fibre

Fish fillets pan-fried with pancetta and caper herb butter

80g butter, softened
2 tablespoons coarsely chopped fresh flat-leaf parsley
1 tablespoon capers, rinsed, drained
2 cloves garlic, quartered
2 green onions, chopped coarsely
8 slices pancetta (120g)
4 x 150g white fish fillets
1 tablespoon olive oil
350g asparagus, trimmed

1 Blend or process butter, parsley, capers, garlic and onion until mixture forms a smooth paste.
2 Spread 1 heaped tablespoon of the butter mixture and two slices of the pancetta on each fish fillet.
3 Heat oil in large heavy-base frying pan; cook fish, pancetta butter side down, until pancetta is crisp. Turn carefully; cook until cooked as desired.
4 Meanwhile, boil, steam or microwave asparagus until tender.
5 Serve fish and asparagus drizzled with pan juices.

on the table in 25 minutes
serves 4 **per serving** 28.5g total fat (14.1g saturated fat); 11743kJ (417 cal); 1.7g carbohydrate; 38.2g protein; 1.4g fibre

Fish with stir-fried shiitake mushrooms and asian greens

2 teaspoons salt
4 x 200g fish fillets, with skin intact
¼ cup (60ml) vegetable oil
500g baby buk choy, chopped coarsely
500g choy sum, chopped coarsely
100g shiitake mushrooms, sliced thinly
125g crab meat
2 tablespoons mirin
⅓ cup (80ml) soy sauce
⅓ cup (80ml) fish stock

1 Sprinkle salt on skin of fish. Heat 1 tablespoon of the oil in wok; cook fish, skin-side down, in batches, until browned both sides and cooked as desired. Cover to keep warm.
2 Heat wok; stir-fry buk choy and choy sum until just wilted. Add mushrooms, crab and another tablespoon of the oil; stir-fry 1 minute. Add remaining oil with mirin, sauce and stock; stir-fry until heated through.
3 Divide vegetables among serving plates; top with fish, drizzle with sauce.

on the table in 20 minutes
serves 4 **per serving** 19g total fat (3.2g saturated fat); 1668kJ (399 cal); 3.9g carbohydrate; 49.8g protein; 3.9g fibre

Fish and spinach with olive basil sauce

750g spinach, trimmed, chopped coarsely
⅓ cup (80ml) extra virgin olive oil
4 x 200g white fish fillets
1 tablespoon lemon juice
¼ teaspoon dried chilli flakes
1 clove garlic, crushed
⅓ cup (50g) seeded kalamata olives
¼ cup finely shredded fresh basil

1 Boil, steam or microwave spinach until just wilted; drain. Cover to keep warm.
2 Meanwhile, heat 1 tablespoon of the oil in large frying pan; cook fish until browned both sides and cooked as desired. Remove from pan; cover to keep warm.
3 Place remaining oil in same cleaned pan; cook remaining ingredients, stirring, until heated through. Divide spinach among serving plates; top with fish and olive basil sauce.

on the table in 15 minutes
serves 4 **per serving** 23.1g total fat (4g saturated fat); 1676kJ (401 cal); 3.6g carbohydrate; 43.4g protein; 3g fibre

Deep-fried perch with chilli lime dressing

3 lebanese cucumbers (390g)
3 medium carrots (360g)
4 x 400g whole ocean perch, cleaned
vegetable oil, for deep-frying
½ cup (75g) plain flour
2 teaspoons salt
2 teaspoons ground white pepper
chilli lime dressing
⅓ cup (80ml) sweet chilli sauce
2 teaspoons fish sauce
¼ cup (60ml) lime juice
1 teaspoon sesame oil
2 tablespoons coarsely chopped thai basil
2 tablespoons coarsely chopped vietnamese mint
2 tablespoons water

1 Using vegetable peeler, slice cucumbers and carrots lengthways into thin strips; combine in medium bowl.
2 Make chilli lime dressing.
3 Discard fish heads; score each fish three times both sides.
4 Heat vegetable oil in wok. Combine flour, salt and pepper in medium shallow bowl; coat fish in flour mixture. Deep-fry fish, in two batches, until browned lightly and cooked through; drain on absorbent paper.
5 Divide carrot mixture among plates; top with fish, drizzle with dressing.
chilli lime dressing place ingredients in screw-top jar; shake well.

on the table in 35 minutes
serves 4 **per serving** 18.5g total fat (2.4g saturated fat); 1814kJ (434 cal); 24.3g carbohydrate; 39.4g protein; 5.5g fibre

Salmon with peas and green onion

60g butter
4 x 200g salmon fillets
2 cloves garlic, crushed
2 medium brown onions (300g), sliced thinly
¾ cup (180ml) fish stock
2 tablespoons lemon juice
1½ cups (185g) frozen peas
8 green onions, trimmed, cut into 4cm pieces
1 tablespoon finely grated lemon rind
1 teaspoon sea salt flakes

1 Melt half of the butter in large heated frying pan; cook salmon until browned both sides. Remove from pan; cover to keep warm.
2 Melt remaining butter in same pan; cook garlic and brown onion, stirring, until onion softens. Add stock, juice, peas and green onion; bring to a boil. Reduce heat, simmer, uncovered, 2 minutes.
3 Return salmon to pan; sprinkle with rind and salt. Cook, uncovered, until salmon is cooked as desired.

on the table in 30 minutes
serves 4 **per serving** 26.9g total fat (11.4g saturated fat); 1918kJ (459 cal); 8.5g carbohydrate; 43.8g protein; 4.5g fibre

Fish curry with coriander and snake beans

80g ghee
½ small brown onion (40g), chopped finely
3 cloves garlic, crushed
4cm piece fresh ginger (20g), grated
1 fresh long red chilli, sliced thinly
½ teaspoon ground tumeric
1½ teaspoons sweet paprika
2 teaspoons ground coriander
1 cup (250ml) coconut milk
½ cup (125ml) water
2 teaspoons tamarind concentrate
1 teaspoon salt
250g snake beans, cut into 5cm lengths
700g white fish fillets, chopped coarsely
½ cup loosely packed fresh coriander leaves

1 Heat ghee in large saucepan; cook onion, garlic and ginger, stirring, until soft. Add chilli; cook, stirring 1 minute. Add spices; cook, stirring over low heat, about 5 minutes or until fragrant.
2 Add coconut milk, water, tamarind and salt; bring to a boil. Add beans and fish; simmer, uncovered, about 5 minutes or until fish is just cooked.
3 Top curry with coriander and serve with steamed basmati rice and pappadums, if desired.

on the table in 30 minutes
serves 4 **per serving** 37.1g total fat (25.7g saturated fat); 2161kJ (517 cal); 5.3g carbohydrate; 39.6g protein; 3.8g fibre

Fish with chermoulla

3 cloves garlic, crushed
1 teaspoon ground cumin
½ teaspoon hot paprika
2 tablespoons coarsely chopped fresh coriander
2 tablespoons coarsely chopped fresh flat-leaf parsley
¼ cup (60ml) olive oil
¼ cup (60ml) lemon juice
2 teaspoons finely grated lemon rind
8 x 150g white fish steaks

1 Combine garlic, spices, herbs, oil, juice and rind in large non-metallic bowl; remove and reserve half of the chermoulla mixture. Place fish in large bowl; toss to coat in remaining chermoulla. Cover; refrigerate 15 minutes.
2 Remove fish, discard marinado. Cook fish in large heated oiled frying pan until browned both sides and cooked as desired. Serve fish drizzled with reserved chermoulla.

on the table in 35 minutes
serves 8 **per serving** 10.2g total fat (2g saturated fat); 907kJ (217 cal); 0.4g carbohydrate; 30.8g protein; 0.3g fibre
tip chermoulla is a spicy Moroccan marinade which can also be served as a sauce. If hot paprika is unavailable, substitute it with ½ teaspoon of sweet paprika and a hearty pinch of cayenne pepper.

Moroccan fillets with fruity couscous

4 x 200g white fish fillets
1 clove garlic, crushed
1cm piece fresh ginger (5g), grated
1 teaspoon ground cumin
½ teaspoon ground turmeric
½ teaspoon hot paprika
½ teaspoon ground coriander
1 tablespoon olive oil
fruity couscous
2 cups (400g) couscous
2 cups (500ml) boiling water
50g butter
1 large pear (330g), chopped finely
½ cup (75g) finely chopped dried apricots
½ cup (95g) coarsely chopped dried figs
½ cup coarsely chopped fresh flat-leaf parsley
¼ cup (40g) toasted pine nuts

1 Combine fish, garlic, ginger and spices in large bowl.
2 Heat oil in large frying pan; cook fish, in batches, until browned both sides and cooked as desired.
3 Meanwhile, make fruity couscous.
4 Divide couscous among serving plates; top with fish. Accompany with a bowl of combined yogurt and coarsely chopped fresh coriander, if desired.
fruity couscous place couscous, the water and butter in large heatproof bowl. Cover; stand about 5 minutes or until water is absorbed, fluffing with fork occasionally. Stir in remaining ingredients.

on the table in 35 minutes
serves 4 **per serving** 27.1g total fat (9.3g saturated fat); 3875kJ (927 cal); 108.1g carbohydrate; 57.1g protein; 8.9g fibre

Baby octopus and eggplant in tomato and caper sauce

1 tablespoon olive oil
1.2kg whole cleaned baby octopus
1 clove garlic, sliced thinly
3 shallots (75g), sliced thinly
4 baby eggplants (240g), sliced thinly
1 medium red capsicum (200g), sliced thinly
½ cup (125ml) dry red wine
700g bottled tomato pasta sauce
⅓ cup (80ml) water
¼ cup (40g) drained baby capers, rinsed
2 tablespoons coarsely chopped fresh oregano

1 Heat half of the oil in large deep frying pan; cook octopus, in batches, until just changed in colour and tender. Cover to keep warm.
2 Heat remaining oil in same pan; cook garlic and shallot, stirring, until shallot softens. Add eggplant and capsicum; cook, stirring, about 5 minutes or until vegetables are just tender.
3 Add wine, sauce, the water and octopus, bring to a boil. Reduce heat, simmer, covered, about 10 minutes or until sauce thickens slightly. Stir in capers and oregano. Top with extra oregano leaves and serve with steamed white long-grain rice, if desired.

on the table in 35 minutes
serves 4 **per serving** 8.2g total fat (0.8g saturated fat); 1701kJ (407 cal); 21.4g carbohydrate; 53.4g protein; 5.4g fibre

Spiced fish with lemon yogurt sauce

2 cups (400g) long-grain white rice
1 medium lemon (140g), sliced thinly
1 teaspoon ground cumin
1 teaspoon ground cinnamon
2 teaspoons hot paprika
1 tablespoon plain flour
4 x 150g white fish fillets
1 tablespoon olive oil
400g baby carrots
¾ cup (200g) low-fat yogurt
1 tablespoon lemon juice
2 tablespoons coarsely chopped fresh coriander

1 Cook rice in large saucepan of boiling water, uncovered, until tender; drain.
2 Meanwhile, heat large oiled frying pan; cook lemon, uncovered, until lightly browned both sides. Remove from pan.
3 Combine spices and flour in small bowl; sprinkle over fish.
4 Heat oil in same pan; cook fish, uncovered, until browned both sides and cooked as desired.
5 Meanwhile, boil, steam or microwave carrots until just tender; drain.
6 Combine yogurt, juice and coriander in small bowl. Serve fish on rice with lemon, carrots and yogurt mixture.

on the table in 30 minutes
serves 4 **per serving** 8.6g total fat (1.8g saturated fat); 2579kJ (617 cal); 89.2g carbohydrate; 41.3g protein; 5.8g fibre

Kedgeree

1 tablespoon vegetable oil
1 medium brown onion (150g), chopped finely
1 tablespoon mild curry paste
3 cups cooked long-grain white rice
415g can pink salmon, drained, flaked
¼ cup (60ml) cream
1 hard-boiled egg
2 tablespoons chopped fresh flat-leaf parsley

1 Heat oil in large saucepan; cook onion, stirring, until soft. Add curry paste; cook, stirring, until fragrant. Stir in rice, salmon and cream; cook, stirring, until hot.
2 Cut egg into eight wedges and gently stir through kedgeree; sprinkle with parsley to serve.

on the table in 20 minutes
serves 4 **per serving** 25.1g total fat (8.4g saturated fat); 2536kJ (846 cal); 121g carbohydrate; 31.1g protein; 2.4g fibre
tip you will need approximately 1¼ cups (250g) of uncooked long-grain rice for this recipe.

Fish with raisin almond rice

50g butter
1 medium onion (150g), chopped finely
1 cup green apple (130g), peeled, chopped finely
1 cup (200g) wild blend rice
1½ cups (375ml) chicken stock
2 tablespoons raisins
½ cup coarsely chopped fresh flat-leaf parsley
¼ cup (35g) slivered almonds, toasted
4 x 200g white fish steaks
lemon wedges, for serving

1 Melt half of the butter in medium saucepan; cook onion and
apple, stirring, without browning, until softened. Stir in rice to coat
in butter mixture.
2 Stir in stock; bring to a boil. Simmer, covered, about 12 minutes,
until stock is absorbed. Remove from heat; stand, covered, 5 minutes.
Stir in raisins, parsley and almonds.
3 Meanwhile, melt remaining butter in large frying pan; cook fish
about 2 minutes each side or until browned and just cooked through.
4 Serve with rice mixture and lemon wedges.

on the table in 35 minutes
serves 4 **per serving** 20.3g total fat (8.7g saturated fat); 2383kJ
(570 cal); 46.7g carbohydrate; 47.9g protein; 3.4g fibre
tips wild blend rice is a combination of white long grain rice and wild rice.
Rice can be prepared several hours ahead; cook fish just before serving.

Salmon and fennel spaghetti

375g spaghetti
1 tablespoon olive oil
4 baby fennel bulbs (300g), sliced thinly
2 tablespoons (30g) drained capers
½ cup (125ml) dry white wine
1 teaspoon finely grated lime rind
1 tablespoon lime juice
250g smoked salmon
200g crème fraîche
250g baby spinach leaves
¼ cup finely chopped fresh chives

1 Cook pasta in large saucepan of boiling water, uncovered, until just tender; drain.
2 Meanwhile, heat oil in medium frying pan; cook fennel and capers, uncovered, until fennel softens. Add wine, rind and juice; bring to a boil. Reduce heat, simmer, uncovered, about 5 minutes or until liquid reduces by half.
3 Slice salmon, against the grain, into small pieces; combine with hot pasta and fennel mixture in large bowl. Gently stir in crème fraîche and spinach; sprinkle with chives.

on the table in 25 minutes
serves 4 **per serving** 28.6g total fat (14.4g saturated fat); 2822kJ (675 cal); 68g carbohydrate; 28.1g protein; 6.2g fibre

Fish provençale with herbed fresh tomatoes

2 medium yellow zucchini (240g), quartered lengthways
3 medium green zucchini (360g), quartered lengthways
12 tiny new potatoes (480g)
¼ cup (60ml) olive oil
4 x 150g white fish fillets
2 medium egg tomatoes (150g), seeded, chopped finely
2 tablespoons lemon juice
1 tablespoon coarsely chopped fresh dill
1 tablespoon coarsely chopped fresh flat-leaf parsley
1 tablespoon coarsely chopped fresh tarragon

1 Boil, steam or microwave both zucchini and potatoes, separately, until just tender; drain.
2 Meanwhile, heat 2 teaspoons of the oil in medium frying pan; cook fish, uncovered, until browned both sides and cooked as desired. Remove from pan; cover to keep warm.
3 Heat remaining oil in same cleaned pan; cook tomato and juice, stirring, until just hot. Remove from heat; stir in herbs. Serve vegetables with fish, tomato mixture and lemon wedges, if desired.

on the table in 30 minutes
serves 4 **per serving** 17.6g total fat (3g saturated fat); 1630kJ (390 cal); 19.1g carbohydrate; 36.1g protein; 3.4g fibre

Fish fillets with lemon caper butter

2 medium zucchini (240g)
2 medium carrots (240g)
80g butter
4 x 150g bream fillets, skin on
1 tablespoon plain flour
¼ cup (60ml) lemon juice
2 teaspoons drained baby capers
2 tablespoons finely chopped fresh flat-leaf parsley

1 Using a vegetable peeler, slice zucchini and carrots lengthways into thin strips.
2 Melt 20g of the butter in large frying pan; cook zucchini and carrot, turning occasionally, until vegetables are just tender. Remove from pan; cover to keep warm.
3 Lightly dust skin-side only of fish with flour.
4 Melt half of the remaining butter in same pan; cook fish, skin-side down, covered, until just cooked through. Remove from pan; cover to keep warm.
5 Add remaining butter to cleaned pan; cook, over low heat, until butter browns. Add juice, capers and parsley; stir until combined.
6 Serve fish on vegetable strips with browned butter sauce.

on the table in 25 minutes
serves 4 **per serving** 24.4g total fat (13.5g saturated fat); 1559kJ (373 cal); 6.5g carbohydrate; 31.1g protein; 2.7g fibre

Seafood rice

30g butter
500g marinara mix
1 tablespoon olive oil
1 clove garlic, crushed
200g button mushrooms, sliced thinly
100g snow peas, sliced thinly
4 green onions, chopped finely
4 slices smoked salmon (75g), chopped coarsely
4 cups cooked rice
2 tablespoons chopped fresh flat-leaf parsley
¼ cup (60ml) lemon juice
¼ cup (20g) grated parmesan cheese

1 Heat butter in large frying pan; cook marinara mix, stirring, until tender. Remove from pan.
2 Heat oil in same pan; cook garlic, mushrooms and snow peas, stirring, until snow peas are tender.
3 Return marinara mix to pan, add onion, salmon, rice, parsley and juice; stir until heated through. Serve sprinkled with cheese.

on the table in 30 minutes
serves 4 **per serving** 17.5g total fat (6.9g saturated fat); 2391kJ (572 cal); 56.8g carbohydrate; 44.3g protein; 3.8g fibre
tip you will need about 1⅓ cups (265g) of uncooked rice for this recipe.

Salt and pepper salmon cutlets with daikon and snow pea salad

4 x 265g salmon cutlets
2 teaspoons sea salt
1 teaspoon freshly ground black pepper
1 tablespoon peanut oil
½ small daikon (200g)
150g snow pea sprouts
200g snow peas, sliced thinly
1 fresh long red chilli, sliced thinly
½ cup loosely packed thai basil leaves
½ cup loosely packed vietnamese mint leaves
2 small pink grapefruit (460g)
chilli lime vinaigrette
2 tablespoons sweet chilli sauce
2 tablespoons lime juice
1 tablespoon rice vinegar
1 tablespoon finely chopped fresh lemon grass
1 clove garlic, crushed
2 teaspoons brown sugar

1 Make chilli lime vinaigrette.
2 Combine fish, salt and pepper in large bowl. Heat oil in large frying pan; cook fish, in batches, until browned both sides and cooked as desired.
3 Meanwhile, slice daikon thinly lengthways; cut slices into thin sticks. Combine daikon in large bowl with sprouts, snow peas, chilli and herbs.
4 Segment grapefruit over salad to save juice; discard membranes from segments. Add segments and half of the vinaigrette to salad; toss gently to combine.
5 Divide salad among serving plates; top with fish, drizzle with remaining vinaigrette.
chilli lime vinaigrette place ingredients in screw-top jar; shake well.

on the table in 35 minutes
serves 4 **per serving** 20.7g total fat (4.4g saturated fat); 1973kJ (472 cal); 20.8g carbohydrate; 47.7g protein; 5.5g fibre

Quick fish curry

750g white fish fillets, chopped coarsely
1 fresh long red chilli, chopped finely
1 tablespoon lime juice
½ teaspoon salt
1 tablespoon vegetable oil
1 medium brown onion (150g), sliced thinly
4cm piece fresh ginger (20g), grated
2 cloves garlic, crushed
1 tablespoon mild curry paste
140ml can coconut cream
½ cup firmly packed fresh coriander leaves
1 lime, cut into wedges

1 Toss fish in combined chilli, juice and salt.
2 Heat oil in medium frying pan; cook onion, stirring, until soft. Add ginger, garlic and curry paste; cook stirring, until fragrant.
3 Add coconut cream, bring to a boil. Reduce heat, simmer, uncovered, until sauce thickens slightly. Add fish, cook, covered, about 5 minutes or until fish is just cooked through.
4 Sprinkle fish curry with coriander leaves. Serve with lime wedges, rice and green beans, if desired.

on the table in 30 minutes
serves 4 **per serving** 17.9g total fat (8.4g saturated fat); 1442kJ (345 cal); 4.6g carbohydrate; 40.2g protein; 2.5g fibre

Steamed fish with black bean and chilli sauce

500g gai lan, cut into 8cm lengths
4 x 200g white fish fillets
1 tablespoon black bean garlic sauce
1 tablespoon water
5cm piece fresh ginger (25g), sliced thinly
1 tablespoon peanut oil
2 fresh small red thai chillies, sliced thinly

1 Line bamboo steamer with a plate large enough to just fit steamer. Place stems of gai lan in single layer on plate. Steam, covered tightly, over wok or pan of boiling water about 3 minutes.
2 Remove lid from steamer, place gai lan leaves then fish on top of stems. Spread with combined sauce and the water, sprinkle with ginger; replace lid; steam about 5 minutes or until fish is just cooked through.
3 Meanwhile, place oil and chilli in small microwave-safe jug; cook on HIGH (100%) for 30 seconds until hot.
4 Serve fish on gai lan; drizzle with hot oil mixture. Serve with steamed rice or noodles, if desired.

on the table in 15 minutes
serves 4 **per serving** 9.2g total fat (2.3g saturated fat); 1175kJ (281 cal); 2.7g carbohydrate; 44.1g protein; 4.9g fibre

Crispy fish with asian greens

8 whiting fillets (960g)
¼ cup (35g) cornflour
vegetable oil, for deep-frying
500g gai lan
¼ cup (60ml) oyster sauce
2 teaspoons sesame oil
2 green onions, sliced thinly
½ cup firmly packed fresh coriander leaves
1 fresh long red chilli, sliced thinly

1 Toss fish in cornflour; shake away excess. Heat oil in wok; add fish and cook until browned and cooked through. Drain fish on absorbent paper.
2 Meanwhile, cut gai lan into 8cm lengths. Boil, steam or microwave gai lan until just tender; drain well.
3 Arrange gai lan on serving plates, drizzle with combined oyster sauce and sesame oil; top with fish, sprinkle with onions, coriander and chilli. Serve with steamed rice, if desired.

on the table in 25 minutes
serves 4 **per serving** 17.6g total fat (2.5g saturated fat); 1789kJ (428 cal); 13.6g carbohydrate; 51.3g protein; 4.9g fibre

Salmon fillets with wasabi and coriander butter

500g kipfler potatoes, halved
30g butter
¼ cup (60ml) olive oil
4 x 200g salmon fillets
2 teaspoons coriander seeds, crushed
lime wedges, for serving
wasabi and coriander butter
100g butter, softened
1 tablespoon wasabi paste
1 clove garlic, crushed
¼ cup firmly packed fresh coriander leaves

1 Boil, steam or microwave potatoes until tender; drain.
2 Meanwhile, heat butter and 1 tablespoon of the oil in large frying pan over high heat until butter begins to foam. Cook salmon, skin-side down, uncovered, about 3 minutes or until skin is crisp. Reduce heat, cover pan with lid; cook for further few minutes or until salmon is cooked as desired. Remove salmon from pan; cover to keep warm.
3 Heat remaining oil in medium frying pan; cook potatoes, shaking pan occasionally, about 5 minutes or until browned all over. Add coriander seeds; cook until fragrant.
4 Meanwhile, make wasabi and coriander butter.
5 Serve salmon on potatoes with wasabi and coriander butter and lime wedges.
wasabi and coriander butter using wooden spoon, beat butter, wasabi and garlic in small bowl until combined. Stir in coriander.

on the table in 35 minutes
serves 4 **per serving** 54.7g total fat (22.7g saturated fat); 3051kJ (703 cal); 16.9g carbohydrate; 42.9g protein; 3g fibre

Mussels with white wine and vegetables

2kg black mussels
30g butter
1 medium brown onion (150g), chopped finely
1 medium carrot (120g), chopped finely
1 trimmed celery stalk (100g), chopped finely
1 clove garlic, crushed
½ cup (125ml) dry white wine
8 slices crusty bread
1 tablespoon olive oil
½ cup chopped fresh flat-leaf parsley

1 Scrub mussels; remove beards.
2 Heat butter in large saucepan; cook onion, carrot, celery and garlic, stirring, until onion is soft.
3 Add wine to pan; bring to a boil. Add mussels; cook, covered, 5 minutes or until mussels open (discard any that do not).
4 Meanwhile, brush bread with oil and grill until toasted on both sides.
5 Sprinkle mussels and broth with parsley; serve with toast.

on the table in 30 minutes
serves 4 **per serving** 4.8g total fat (1.9g saturated fat); 790kJ (189 cal); 10.6g carbohydrate; 6g protein; 1.2g fibre
tips use a stiff brush to scrub the mussels under cold water. Keep the shell, still hinged, from the first mussel you eat and use this to remove the remaining mussels from their shells.

Cajun-style blackened fish with green rice

20g butter
1 small green capsicum (150g), chopped finely
1½ cups (300g) basmati rice
3 cups (750ml) chicken stock
60g butter, melted, extra
1 green onion, chopped finely
1 tablespoon lemon juice
4 x 200g white fish steaks
1 tablespoon cajun spice mix
8 green onions, chopped finely, extra
½ cup finely chopped fresh flat-leaf parsley
1 teaspoon cracked black pepper

1 Heat butter in medium saucepan; cook capsicum, stirring, until softened.
2 Meanwhile, place the rice in sieve, rinse well with cold water. Add rice and stock to pan, bring to a boil, stirring occasionally. Cover pan with tight-fitting lid; reduce heat to as low as possible, cook rice 12 minutes or until cooked as desired.
3 Meanwhile, combine extra butter, onion and juice. Reserve half.
4 Brush one half of the butter mixture over fish; sprinkle with spice mix. Cook fish in large oiled frying pan until blackened on both sides and just cooked through.
5 Stir extra onions, parsley and pepper into the rice.
6 Serve fish with rice, reserved butter mixture and lemon wedges, if desired.

on the table in 30 minutes
serves 4 **per serving** 22.1g total fat (12.7g saturated fat); 2725kJ (652 cal); 62.7g carbohydrate; 49g protein; 1.9g fibre

Crispy skin salmon on braised peas and mash

4 medium potatoes (800g), peeled, chopped
40g butter
4 shallots (100g), sliced thinly
1 cup (250ml) chicken stock
1 cup (120g) frozen peas
1 tablespoon chopped fresh flat-leaf parsley
4 x 200g salmon fillets
salt
1 tablespoon olive oil
½ cup (125ml) milk, warmed
40g butter, extra

1 Boil or steam potato until soft; drain.
2 Meanwhile, heat half of the butter in large saucepan; cook shallots, stirring, until soft. Add stock and frozen peas; simmer, uncovered, until tender. Add parsley, then remaining butter.
3 Rub salmon skin with a little salt. Heat oil in large frying pan. Cook salmon, skin-side down, about 3 minutes or until skin is crisp and browned. Turn; cook further minute or until salmon is cooked as desired.
4 Mash potato with milk and extra butter until smooth.
5 Divide mash among serving plates; spoon pea mixture around mash. Top with salmon, skin-side up.

on the table in 30 minutes
serves 4 **per serving** 37g total fat (15.6g saturated fat); 2746kJ (657 cal); 30.8g carbohydrate; 47.8g protein; 6g fibre

Prawn fritters with avocado salsa

450g cooked large prawns
2 tablespoons olive oil
1 medium brown onion (150g), chopped coarsely
1 clove garlic, crushed
2 teaspoons hot paprika
½ teaspoon ground cumin
¼ teaspoon ground white pepper
¼ teaspoon cayenne pepper
1½ cups (225g) self-raising flour
2 eggs
1½ cups (375ml) milk
1 tablespoon coarsely chopped fresh chives
2 medium avocados (500g), chopped coarsely
2 medium tomatoes (380g), chopped coarsely
1 spring onion (25g), trimmed, sliced thinly
2 tablespoons lime juice

1 Shell and devein prawns; chop prawn flesh coarsely.
2 Heat half of the oil in large frying pan; cook onion, garlic and spices, stirring, until onion softens.
3 Place flour in large bowl; stir in combined eggs and milk, stir until smooth. Stir in chives, onion mixture and prawn.
4 Heat remaining oil in same cleaned frying pan; cook ¼-cups of prawn mixture, in batches, until browned both sides.
5 Meanwhile, combine remaining ingredients in medium bowl. Serve fritters with avocado salsa.

on the table in 30 minutes
serves 4 **per serving** 36.8g total fat (9g saturated fat); 2688kJ (643 cal); 48.9g carbohydrate; 26.9g protein; 5.4g fibre
tips fritter batter can be prepared 4 hours ahead; cover, refrigerate.
You can buy 200g of shelled prawns, if you prefer, for this recipe.

Steamed fish with chilli and ginger

2 baby buk choy (300g), quartered
4 x 200g white fish cutlets
10cm piece fresh ginger (50g), cut into 4cm strips
2 green onions, cut into 4cm strips
¼ cup (60ml) salt-reduced soy sauce
1 teaspoon sesame oil
1 fresh large red chilli, sliced thinly
1 cup loosely packed fresh coriander leaves

1 Place buk choy on large heatproof plate inside steamer; top with fish.
Sprinkle ginger and onion over fish, then spoon over sauce and oil. Cover
steamer; steam fish about 5 minutes or until just cooked through.
2 Serve fish topped with chilli and coriander.

on the table in 20 minutes
serves 4 **per serving** 4.9g total fat (1.3g saturated fat); 823kJ (197 cal);
2.3g carbohydrate; 34.8g protein; 1.8g fibre

Spaghetti with puttanesca sauce

2 tablespoons olive oil
2 cloves garlic, crushed
4 medium tomatoes (760g), chopped coarsely
½ cup chopped fresh flat-leaf parsley
12 stuffed green olives, sliced thinly
45g can anchovy fillets, drained, chopped finely
1 tablespoon finely shredded fresh basil
pinch chilli powder
375g spaghetti

1 Heat oil in medium frying pan; cook garlic until it just changes colour. Add tomato, parsley, olives, anchovy, basil and chilli powder; cook, stirring, 5 minutes.
2 Meanwhile, cook pasta in large saucepan of boiling water until tender; drain. Combine sauce and pasta.

on the table in 30 minutes
serves 4 **per serving** 11.2g total fat (1.6g saturated fat); 2027kJ (458 cal); 70.8g carbohydrate; 14.7g protein; 6.2g fibre

Salmon steaks with fennel salad

4 x 200g salmon steaks
1 tablespoon finely chopped fresh chives
1 tablespoon finely chopped fresh dill
200g baby spinach leaves
2 medium apples (300g), sliced thinly
2 baby fennel bulbs (260g), trimmed, sliced thinly
1 lebanese cucumber (130g), seeded, sliced thinly
½ cup coarsely chopped fresh chives
¼ cup coarsely chopped fresh dill
dressing
2 tablespoons red wine vinegar
1 tablespoon olive oil
2 teaspoons white sugar
2 teaspoons dijon mustard

1 Make dressing.
2 Combine 1 tablespoon of the dressing with fish, finely chopped chives and finely chopped dill in medium bowl.
3 Cook fish in heated oiled large frying pan until cooked as desired.
4 Place remaining ingredients in large bowl with remaining dressing; toss gently to combine. Serve fish with salad.
dressing place ingredients in screw-top jar; shake well.

on the table in 25 minutes
serves 4 **per serving** 19g total fat (3.8g saturated fat); 1587kJ (379 cal); 10.7g carbohydrate; 41.1g protein; 4.1g fibre

Microwave risotto marinara

This quick and easy version of the classic requires no pots or pans –
just one bowl and a microwave oven – so it's the perfect meal for risotto
lovers who have no time to waste.

60g butter
1 small brown onion (80g), sliced thinly
2 cloves garlic, crushed
2 cups (400g) arborio rice
1 litre (4 cups) chicken stock
½ cup (125ml) dry white wine
700g seafood marinara mix
1 tablespoon finely grated lemon rind
¼ cup (60ml) lemon juice
¼ cup coarsely chopped fresh dill
¼ cup coarsely chopped fresh flat-leaf parsley
4 green onions, sliced thinly

1 Place half of the butter, onion and garlic in large microwave-safe bowl;
cook, uncovered, on HIGH (100%) about 2 minutes or until onion softens.
Add rice, stir to coat in butter mixture; cook, uncovered, on HIGH (100%)
1 minute. Stir in stock and wine; cook, uncovered, on HIGH (100%)
15 minutes, pausing to stir every 3 minutes.
2 Stir in marinara mix; cook, uncovered, on HIGH (100%) about 7 minutes
or until seafood has changed in colour and rice is just tender, stirring
once during cooking.
3 Stir in remaining ingredients and remaining butter just before serving.

on the table in 35 minutes
serves 4 **per serving** 19g total fat (10.1g saturated fat); 3148kJ
(753 cal); 84.9g carbohydrate; 53.4g protein; 1.8g fibre

Stir-fried garlic prawns

1.25kg large uncooked king prawns
2 tablespoons olive oil
6 cloves garlic, crushed
2 fresh small red thai chillies, chopped finely
2 tablespoons chopped fresh flat-leaf parsley

1 Shell and devein prawns, leaving tails intact.
2 Heat oil in wok; stir-fry garlic and chilli until fragrant.
3 Add prawns; stir-fry until just changed in colour. Serve sprinkled with parsley. Accompany with lemon wedges, if desired.

on the table in 20 minutes
serves 4 **per serving** 10.2g total fat (1.5g saturated fat); 941kJ (225 cal); 0.5g carbohydrate; 32.4g protein; 0.9g fibre

Salmon with lime and chilli sauce

2 cloves garlic, crushed
1 teaspoon grated lime rind
1cm piece fresh ginger (5g), grated
4 x 200g salmon fillets
20g butter
1 tablespoon peanut oil
8 baby buk choy, halved
⅓ cup (80ml) sweet chilli sauce
¼ cup (60ml) lime juice
2 tablespoons chopped fresh coriander

1 Combine garlic, rind and ginger in small bowl; rub half of the garlic mixture over flesh side of salmon.
2 Heat butter and oil in large frying pan until butter begins to foam. Cook salmon until browned on both sides and cooked as desired. Remove from pan; cover to keep warm.
3 Add buk choy to same pan with remaining garlic mixture, chilli sauce and juice; stir until buk choy is just tender.
4 Sprinkle salmon with coriander and serve with buk choy mixture. Accompany with lime wedges, if desired.

on the table in 20 minutes
serves 4 **per serving** 20g total fat (4.1g saturated fat); 1639kJ (392 cal); 7.5g carbohydrate; 42.9g protein; 5.3g fibre

bakes

Salmon fillo triangles

20g butter
3 green onions, sliced thinly
1 small red capsicum (150g), chopped finely
2 tablespoons plain flour
¼ cup (60ml) milk
½ cup (125ml) cream
1 tablespoon lemon juice
1 tablespoon drained baby capers, rinsed
30g baby spinach leaves
400g can red salmon, drained, flaked
4 sheets fillo pastry
50g butter, melted
150g mesclun
200g cherry tomatoes, halved

1 Preheat oven to 200°C/180°C fan-forced. Oil oven tray.
2 Melt butter in medium frying pan; cook onion and capsicum, stirring, until onion softens. Add flour; cook, stirring, until mixture bubbles. Gradually add combined milk and cream; stir until mixture boils and thickens. Remove from heat; stir in juice, capers, spinach and salmon.
3 Brush one sheet of the fillo with a little of the melted butter; fold in half lengthways. Place a quarter of the salmon mixture at bottom of one narrow edge of fillo, leaving a 1cm border. Fold opposite corner of fillo diagonally across filling to form a triangle; continue folding to end of fillo piece, retaining triangle shape. Place triangle on tray, seam-side down. Repeat with remaining fillo and salmon mixture.
4 Brush triangles with remaining melted butter; bake, uncovered, about 10 minutes or until browned lightly and heated through. Serve salmon triangles with mesclun and tomato.

on the table in 35 minutes
serves 4 **per serving** 38.9g total fat (21.5g saturated fat); 2182kJ (522 cal); 19.4g carbohydrate; 23g protein; 3.1g fibre

Lemon grass and lime fish parcels

The lemon grass in this dish is not eaten, but it produces an amazing aroma and flavour simply by being close to the fish during cooking.

2 stems fresh lemon grass
½ cup chopped fresh coriander
1cm piece fresh ginger (5g), grated
3 cloves garlic, crushed
4 spring onions (100g), sliced thinly
2 fresh small red thai chillies, chopped finely
4 x 200g white fish fillets
1 lime, sliced thinly
1 tablespoon peanut oil

1 Preheat oven to 180°C/160°C fan-forced.
2 Trim lemon grass into 10cm pieces; cut each piece in half lengthways.
3 Combine coriander, ginger, garlic, onion and chilli in small bowl.
4 Divide lemon grass among four pieces of foil; top with fish. Top fish with coriander mixture and lime; drizzle with oil. Fold foil around fish to enclose completely; place on oven tray.
5 Bake parcels about 15 minutes or until fish is cooked as desired.
6 Remove fish from foil and discard lemon grass. Serve with steamed rice and lime slices, if desired.

on the table in 30 minutes
serves 4 **per serving** 9.1g total fat (2.2g saturated fat); 1091kJ (261 cal); 2.1g carbohydrate; 41.6g protein; 1.4g fibre
tip wrap fish in blanched banana leaves instead of foil, if desired. They are available in Asian food shops, greengrocers and supermarkets.

Salmon baked in paper with preserved lemon and herbs

8 x 200g salmon fillets, skin removed
½ cup (125ml) extra virgin olive oil
2 tablespoons chopped fresh mint
2 tablespoons chopped fresh coriander
2 tablespoons chopped flat-leaf parsley
2 tablespoons finely sliced preserved lemon
lemon wedges for serving

1 Preheat oven to 200°C/180°C fan-forced.
2 Place each fillet on 30cm square sheet of baking paper. Drizzle with oil; sprinkle with herbs and preserved lemon. Fold paper over to enclose salmon, secure with toothpicks; place on oven tray.
3 Bake salmon about 10 minutes or until cooked as desired.
4 Serve salmon with lemon wedges.

on the table in 30 minutes
serves 8 **per serving** 28.5g total fat (5.2g saturated fat); 1726kJ (413 cal); 0.3g carbohydrate; 39.2g protein; 0.5g fibre
tip salmon can be wrapped in baking paper several hours ahead; bake close to serving.

Cajun-spiced fish with roasted corn salsa

1 clove garlic, crushed
20g butter, melted
2 teaspoons sweet paprika
½ teaspoon ground cumin
1 teaspoon ground white pepper
¼ teaspoon cayenne pepper
4 x 200g white fish fillets
3 trimmed fresh corn cobs (750g)
1 small red onion (100g), chopped coarsely
1 medium avocado (250g), chopped coarsely
250g cherry tomatoes, halved
2 tablespoons lime juice
¼ cup coarsely chopped fresh coriander

1 Preheat oven to 220°C/200°C fan-forced.
2 Combine garlic and butter in small jug; combine spices in small bowl.
3 Place fish on oven tray, brush both sides with garlic mixture, sprinkle with combined spices. Roast, uncovered, about 15 minutes or until browned both sides and cooked as desired.
4 Meanwhile, roast corn on heated lightly oiled grill plate (or grill or barbecue) until browned all over. When corn is just cool enough to handle, cut kernels from cobs with a small, sharp knife.
5 Combine corn kernels in medium bowl with remaining ingredients. Serve fish with salsa.

on the table in 35 minutes
serves 4 **per serving** 18g total fat (4g saturated fat); 1986kJ (475 cal); 25.6g carbohydrate; 48.3g protein; 8.4g fibre

Smoked salmon, caper and dill frittata

6 eggs
½ cup (125ml) cream
1 teaspoon finely grated lemon rind
1 small red onion (100g), sliced thinly
½ cup coarsely chopped fresh dill
2 tablespoons drained baby capers, rinsed
200g sliced smoked salmon

1 Preheat oven to 180°C/160°C fan-forced. Oil deep 20cm square cake pan; line base and sides with baking paper.
2 Whisk eggs, cream and rind in medium bowl; combine onion, dill and capers in small bowl.
3 Spread one-third of the onion mixture into pan; top with half of the salmon then pour half of the egg mixture over salmon. Place half of the remaining onion mixture and remaining salmon in pan. Sprinkle remaining onion mixture over salmon then pour in remaining egg mixture.
4 Bake, uncovered, about 30 minutes or until set. Stand frittata 5 minutes before cutting.

on the table in 35 minutes
serves 4 **per serving** 21.7g total fat (10.4g saturated fat); 1229kJ (294 cal); 2.8g carbohydrate; 22.5g protein; 0.5g fibre

Asian-spiced salmon with nashi, mint and coriander salad

cooking-oil spray
2 teaspoons sichuan peppercorns, crushed
2 star anise
1 tablespoon soy sauce
2 tablespoons honey
4 x 200g salmon fillets
2 medium nashi (400g), sliced thinly
1 fresh long red chilli, sliced thinly
1 medium red onion (170g), sliced thinly
2 green onions, sliced thinly
¾ cup loosely packed fresh mint leaves
¾ cup loosely packed fresh coriander leaves
sesame soy dressing
2 tablespoons soy sauce
¼ cup (60ml) mirin
2 teaspoons caster sugar
¼ teaspoon sesame oil

1 Preheat oven to 180°C/160°C fan-forced. Line large shallow baking dish with foil, extending foil 5cm above long sides of dish; coat lightly with cooking-oil spray.
2 Dry-fry spices in small frying pan until fragrant. Add sauce and honey; bring to a boil. Reduce heat, simmer, uncovered, 2 minutes.
3 Place fish in baking dish; brush both sides with spice mixture. Bake, uncovered, about 15 minutes or until cooked as desired.
4 Meanwhile, make sesame soy dressing.
5 Place remaining ingredients in large bowl with dressing; toss gently to combine. Serve salad with fish.
sesame soy dressing place ingredients in screw-top jar; shake well.

on the table in 35 minutes
serves 4 **per serving** 17.5g total fat (3.7g saturated fat); 1864kJ (446 cal); 26.7g carbohydrate; 45.5g protein; 4g fibre
tip if nashi are not available, substitute with crisp green apples.

Baby leek and fennel fish parcels with fried cauliflower

4 x 200g firm white fillets, with skin
½ medium fennel bulb (150g), trimmed, sliced thinly
4 baby leeks (320g), quartered lengthways
30g butter, melted
vegetable oil for deep-frying
1 medium cauliflower (1.5kg), cut into florets

1 Preheat oven to 200°C/180°C fan-forced.
2 Place each fillet on a square of lightly oiled foil large enough to completely enclose fish; top each fillet with a quarter of the fennel and a quarter of the leek, drizzle with butter. Gather corners of foil squares together above fish; twist to enclose securely.
3 Place parcels on oven tray; bake about 15 minutes or until fish is cooked as desired.
4 Meanwhile, heat oil in wok; deep-fry cauliflower, in batches, until browned and crisp. Drain on absorbent paper.
5 Discard foil from parcels just before serving fish on cauliflower.

on the table in 35 minutes
serves 4 **per serving** 28.1g total fat (7.6g saturated fat); 2098kJ (502 cal); 9.5g carbohydrate; 49.3g protein; 7.9g fibre
tip when deep-frying the cauliflower, make sure the oil is very hot so it crisps and browns. If not, the cauliflower will absorb excess oil and become limp and soggy.

Oven-steamed ocean trout

4 x 200g ocean trout fillets
2 tablespoons lemon juice
1 tablespoon drained capers, chopped coarsely
2 teaspoons coarsely chopped fresh dill
1.2kg large new potatoes, sliced thickly

1 Preheat oven to 200°C/180°C fan-forced.
2 Place each fillet on a square of foil large enough to completely enclose fish; top each fillet with equal amounts of juice, capers and dill. Gather corners of foil squares together above fish, twist to close securely.
3 Place parcels on oven tray; bake about 15 minutes or until fish is cooked as desired. Unwrap and remove fish from foil before serving.
4 Meanwhile, boil, steam or microwave potato until tender. Serve fish with potato.

on the table in 25 minutes
serves 4 **per serving** 7.9g total fat (1.8g saturated fat); 1751kJ (418 cal); 39g carbohydrate; 45.2g protein; 5.8g fibre
tip use tweezers to remove any bones from fish.

Roasted mediterranean-style fish and vegetables

2 x 425g cans whole new potatoes, rinsed, drained
250g cherry tomatoes
1 whole garlic bulb, separated into unpeeled cloves
2 large red onions (600g), chopped coarsely
3 rosemary sprigs, chopped coarsely
¼ cup (60ml) olive oil
8 x 75g skinless bream fillets
¼ cup (60ml) lemon juice
¼ cup firmly packed fresh basil leaves

1 Preheat oven to 220°C/200°C fan forced. Oil large baking dish.
2 Place potatoes and tomatoes in baking dish; crush tomatoes slightly with potato masher. Scatter garlic, onion and rosemary over potatoes; drizzle with half of the oil. Roast, uncovered, 15 minutes.
3 Place fish on vegetables, sprinkle with juice and remaining oil. Bake, uncovered, a further 10 minutes or until fish is cooked as desired. Sprinkle with basil leaves.

on the table in 30 minutes
serves 4 **per serving** 17.6g total fat (3g saturated fat); 1797kJ (430 cal); 27.5g carbohydrate; 36.8g protein; 7.1g fibre

Salmon 'confit' with fennel and herbs

4 x 200g salmon fillets
sea salt flakes
freshly ground black pepper
2 cloves garlic, sliced thinly
3 cups (750ml) extra virgin olive oil, approximately
2 small fennel bulbs (400g), sliced thinly
½ cup (125ml) dry white wine
1 tablespoon grated lemon rind
2 tablespoons chopped fresh fennel tops
2 tablespoons chopped fresh chervil

1 Preheat oven to 120°C/100°C fan-forced.
2 Place salmon in small ovenproof dish, just large enough to fit. Sprinkle with salt, pepper and garlic; add enough oil to cover salmon completely.
3 Bake salmon, uncovered, about 15 minutes or until cooked as desired. The salmon doesn't change colour after cooking time as it is at a low temperature. Remove salmon from dish; drain on absorbent paper.
4 Heat 2 tablespoons of the salmon cooking oil in medium frying pan; cook fennel, stirring, about 5 minutes or until softened. Add wine and rind; cook 5 minutes or until wine is reduced by half. Stir in herbs.
5 Divide fennel mixture among plates, top with salmon. Garnish with extra fresh chervil, if desired.

on the table in 25 minutes
serves 4 **per serving** 25.3g total fat (4.8g saturated fat); 1781kJ (426 cal); 3.4g carbohydrate; 40.1g protein; 3g fibre
tip although this recipe uses a lot of olive oil, it can be strained into a bottle, refrigerated, and used for cooking other fish or seafood.

Roasted ocean trout and asian greens

8 x 100g ocean trout fillets
2 kaffir lime leaves, shredded finely
2 tablespoons finely chopped fresh lemon grass
1 teaspoon sesame oil
250g baby buk choy, quartered
250g choy sum, chopped coarsely
2 teaspoons light soy sauce
⅓ cup (80ml) sweet chilli sauce
¼ cup (60ml) lime juice

1 Preheat oven to 150°C/130°C fan-forced.
2 Place four fish fillets, skin-side down, on board; sprinkle with lime leaves and lemon grass. Top with remaining fish fillets, skin-side up; tie with kitchen string.
3 Place fish in large shallow baking dish; bake, uncovered, 15 minutes.
4 Meanwhile, heat oil in wok; stir-fry buk choy, choy sum and soy sauce until vegetables just wilt.
5 Serve fish with stir-fried vegetables; drizzle with combined chilli sauce and juice.

on the table in 35 minutes
serves 4 **per serving** 9.6g total fat (2.1g saturated fat); 1158kJ (277 cal); 5.4g carbohydrate; 40.6g protein; 2.6g fibre

Baked fish with tomatoes, olives and garlic bread

2 medium green capsicums (400g)
2 tablespoons olive oil
1 small brown onion (80g), chopped finely
1 clove garlic, crushed
1 fresh long red chilli, chopped finely
400g can whole peeled tomatoes
2/3 cup (100g) green olives
1/2 teaspoon dried oregano leaves
2 tablespoons coarsely chopped fresh flat-leaf parsley
4 x 200g firm white fish fillets
garlic bread
1 french bread stick
60g butter, softened
2 cloves garlic, crushed
1 tablespoon chopped flat-leaf parsley

1 Preheat oven to 220°C/200°C fan-forced.
2 Quarter capsicums, remove seeds and place in small baking dish; brush with half of the oil. Bake 10 minutes.
3 Meanwhile, prepare garlic bread.
4 Heat remaining oil in medium frying pan; cook onion, garlic and chilli, stirring, until onion is soft. Add undrained crushed tomatoes, olives, oregano and parsley. Stir until heated through; remove from heat.
5 Place fish in another oiled small ovenproof dish; pour tomato mixture over fish.
6 Bake fish and bread, with capsicum, further 8 minutes or until fish is cooked through, capsicum tender and bread browned and crisp.
7 Cut bread into pieces. Serve with fish, sauce and capsicum.
garlic bread cut bread in half lengthways. Spread with combined butter, garlic and parsley; place buttered-side up on oven tray.

on the table in 30 minutes
serves 4 **per serving** 27.8g total fat (11g saturated fat); 2383kJ (570 cal); 30.8g carbohydrate; 46.9g protein; 4.4g fibre

Salmon with warm vegetable salad

¼ cup (60ml) olive oil
3 green onions, sliced thinly
2 tablespoons coarsely chopped fresh dill
1kg whole salmon fillet
1 corn cob
1 medium carrot (150g), chopped coarsely
½ cup (60g) frozen peas
170g asparagus, trimmed, chopped coarsely
1 medium tomato (190g), seeded, chopped coarsely
100g baby spinach leaves
425g can baby beetroots, drained, quartered

1 Preheat oven to 180°C/160°C fan-forced. Oil large baking tray.
2 Combine 2 tablespoons of the oil with onion and dill in small bowl; rub over salmon. Place salmon, skin-side down, on tray.
3 Roast salmon, uncovered, about 15 minutes or until it is firm to touch.
4 Meanwhile, cut kernels from corn cob. Heat remaining oil in large frying pan; cook corn, carrot and peas, stirring, until tender. Add asparagus and tomato; cook, stirring, until just tender. Add spinach and beetroot; toss gently to combine.
5 Cut salmon into six pieces; serve on warm salad.

on the table in 30 minutes
serves 6 **per serving** 21.7g total fat (4g saturated fat); 1735kJ (415 cal); 14.3g carbohydrate; 37.8g protein; 6.2g fibre

glossary

artichoke, jerusalem
neither from Jerusalem
nor an artichoke, this
crunchy brown-skinned
tuber tastes a bit like
a water chestnut and
belongs to the sunflower
family. Eat raw in salads
or cooked like potatoes.

bacon rashers also
known as bacon slices;
made from cured and
smoked pork side.

beetroot also known
as beets.

black bean sauce an
Asian cooking sauce
made from salted and
fermented soybeans,
spices and wheat flour.

black beans, salted
fermented soybeans.

breadcrumbs

fresh bread, often white,
processed into crumbs.

packaged prepared
fine-textured, crunchy
white breadcrumbs.

broad beans also
called fava, windsor and
horse beans; available
dried, fresh, canned and
frozen. Fresh should be
peeled twice (discarding
both the outer long
green pod and the
beige-green tough inner
shell); frozen beans
have had pods removed
but not the beige shell.

broccolini a cross
between broccoli and
chinese kale; long
asparagus-like stems
with a long loose floret,
both completely edible.
Resembles broccoli, but
is milder and sweeter.

buk choy also known
as bok choy, pak choi,
chinese white cabbage
or chinese chard; has
a fresh, mild mustard
taste. Use both stems
and leaves. Baby buk
choy, also known as pak
kat farang or shanghai
bok choy, is much
smaller and more tender.

butter we use salted
butter unless stated
otherwise.

caperberries olive-sized
fruit formed after the
buds of the caper bush
have flowered; usually
sold pickled in a vinegar
brine with stalks intact.

capers sold dried
and salted or pickled
in a vinegar brine;
baby capers are also
available, both in brine
or dried in salt. Their
pungent taste adds
piquancy to a classic
steak tartare, tapenade,
sauces and condiments.

capsicum also known
as pepper or bell pepper.

caraway seeds the
small, half-moon-shaped
dried seed; adds a sharp
anise flavour to sweet
and savoury dishes.

cardamom native to
India and used extensively
in its cuisine; available in
pod, seed or ground form.
Has a distinctive aromatic,
sweetly rich flavour and
is one of the world's most
expensive spices.

cayenne pepper is
a thin-fleshed, long,
extremely hot, dried red
chilli, usually ground.

cheese

cream commonly called
philadelphia or philly; a
soft cow-milk cheese
with a fat content ranging
from 14% to 33%.

fetta Greek in origin;
a crumbly textured
goat- or sheep-milk
cheese having a sharp,
salty taste. Ripened and
stored in salted whey.

parmesan also called
parmigiano, parmesan is
a hard, grainy cow-milk
cheese which originated
in the Parma region of
Italy. The curd for this
cheese is salted in brine
for a month before
being aged for up to
2 years, preferably in
humid conditions.

ricotta a soft, sweet,
moist, white cow-milk
cheese with a low fat
content (about 8.5%) and
a slightly grainy texture.

chickpeas also known
as garbanzos.

chilli use rubber gloves
when seeding and
chopping fresh chillies
as they can burn your
skin. We use seeded
chillies in our recipes as
the seeds contain the
heat; use fewer chillies
rather than seeding the lot.

dried flakes also called
crushed chilli; dehydrated
deep-red fine slices and
whole seeds.

powder the Asian variety
is the hottest, made from
dried ground thai chillies;
can be used instead
of fresh chillies in the
proportion of ½ teaspoon

chilli powder to 1 medium chopped fresh red chilli.

red thai also called "scuds"; tiny and very hot.

sweet chilli sauce comparatively mild, fairly sticky and runny bottled sauce made from red chillies, sugar, garlic and white vinegar.

chinese barbecue pork roasted pork fillet with a sweet, sticky coating. Available from Asian food shops or specialty stores.

chorizo sausage of Spanish origin, made of coarsely ground pork and highly seasoned with garlic and chilli.

choy sum also called pakaukeo or flowering cabbage, a member of the buk choy family. Has long stems, light green leaves and yellow flowers; both stems and leaves are edible.

coconut

cream obtained from the first pressing of the coconut flesh alone, without the addition of water. Available in cans and cartons at most supermarkets.

milk not the liquid inside the fruit (coconut water), but the diluted liquid from the second pressing of the white flesh of a mature coconut. Available in cans and cartons at most supermarkets.

shredded unsweetened thin strips of dried coconut flesh.

coriander also known as cilantro, pak chee or chinese parsley; bright-green-leafed herb with a pungent aroma and taste. Coriander seeds are dried and sold whole or ground, and neither form tastes remotely like the fresh leaf.

cornichons French for gherkin, a very small pickled cucumber.

couscous a fine, grain-like cereal product made from semolina; from the countries of North Africa. A semolina flour and water dough is sieved then dehydrated to produce minuscule even-sized pellets of couscous; it is rehydrated by steaming or with the addition of a warm liquid and swells to three or four times its original size.

crème fraiche a mature, naturally fermented cream (minimum fat content 35%) having a velvety texture and slightly tangy, nutty flavour. A French variation of sour cream, it can boil without curdling and is used in sweet and savoury dishes.

cumin also known as zeera or comino and resembles caraway in size; is the dried seed of a plant related to the parsley family.

curly endive also called frisée, a prickly-looking, curly-leafed green vegetable having an edible white heart.

Fairly bitter in flavour (like chicory, with which it is often confused), it is used mainly in salads.

daikon also known as white radish; sweet-flavoured Japanese long, white horseradish. After peeling, eat it raw in salads or shredded as a garnish; also great when sliced or cubed and cooked in stir-fries and casseroles. The flesh is white but the skin can be either white or black; buy those that are firm and unwrinkled from Asian food shops.

egg if recipes call for raw or barely cooked eggs, exercise caution if there is a salmonella problem in your area, particularly in food eaten by children and pregnant women.

eggplant also known as aubergine.

fennel also known as finocchio or anise; a crunchy green vegetable slightly resembling celery. Also the name given to the dried seeds of the plant which have a stronger licorice flavour.

fish sauce called naam pla (Thai) or nuoc naam (Vietnamese); the two are almost identical. Made from pulverised salted fermented fish (most often anchovies); has a pungent smell and strong taste. Available in varying degrees of intensity, so use according to your taste.

five-spice powder ingredients may vary, but is most often a mixture of ground cinnamon, cloves, star anise, sichuan pepper and fennel seeds.

flour, plain also called all-purpose flour.

gai lan also known as gai larn, chinese broccoli and chinese kale; green vegetable appreciated more for its stems than its coarse leaves.

galangal also known as ka or lengkaus if fresh and laos if dried and powdered; a root, similar to ginger in its use. It has a hot-sour ginger-citrusy flavour.

ghee clarified butter; with milk solids removed, this fat can be heated to a high temperature without burning.

ginger

fresh also known as green or root ginger; the thick gnarled root of a tropical plant.

pickled pink or red in colour; available, packaged, from Asian food shops. Pickled paper-thin shavings of ginger in a mixture of vinegar, sugar and natural colouring.

honeydew melon a heavy oval fruit with a pale-green to yellow skin, delicate taste and pale green flesh.

horseradish vegetable with edible green leaves, mainly grown for its long, pungent white root.

Available bottled at the supermarket in two forms: prepared horseradish (preserved grated root) and horseradish cream (a commercial paste of grated horseradish, vinegar, oil and sugar). Cannot be substituted for each other in cooking, but both can be used as table condiments.

kaffir lime leaves also called bai magrood; looks like two glossy dark green leaves joined end to end, forming a rounded hourglass shape. Used fresh or dried in many South East Asian dishes, they are used like bay leaves. Sold fresh, dried or frozen, dried leaves are less potent so double the number if using as a substitute for fresh; a strip of fresh lime peel may be substituted for each kaffir lime leaf.

kecap manis a dark, thick sweet soy sauce.

lebanese cucumber short, slender and thin-skinned. Probably the most popular variety because of its tender, edible skin, tiny, yielding seeds, and sweet, fresh and flavoursome taste.

lemon grass a tall, clumping, lemon-smelling and tasting, sharp-edged aromatic tropical grass; the white lower part of the stem is used.

mayonnaise we use whole-egg mayonnaise.

mesclun pronounced mess-kluhn; also called mixed greens or spring salad mix. A blend of assorted young lettuce and other green leaves.

mint, vietnamese not a mint at all, but a pungent and peppery narrow-leafed member of the buckwheat family. Not confined to Vietnam, it is also called Cambodian mint, pak pai (Thailand), laksa leaf (Indonesia), daun kesom (Singapore) and rau ram (Vietnam).

mirin a Japanese champagne-coloured cooking wine, made of glutinous rice and alcohol. Used expressly for cooking, it should not be confused with sake. A seasoned sweet mirin, manjo mirin, made of water, rice, corn syrup and alcohol, is used in Japanese dipping sauces.

mushrooms

button small, cultivated white mushrooms with a mild flavour.

shiitake, fresh also known as chinese black, forest or golden oak mushrooms. Although cultivated, they have the earthiness and taste of wild mushrooms. Large and meaty, they can be used as a substitute for meat in some Asian vegetarian dishes.

mustard

black seeds also called brown mustard seeds; they are more pungent than the white variety.

dijon also called french; is a pale brown, creamy, distinctively flavoured, fairly mild French mustard.

wholegrain also called seeded. A French-style coarse-grain mustard made from crushed mustard seeds and dijon-style french mustard.

nashi a member of the pear family but resembling an apple with its pale-yellow-green, tennis-ball-sized appearance; commonly called the Asian pear.

noodles

dried rick stick made from rice flour and water, available flat and wide or very thin (vermicelli). Must be soaked in boiling water to soften.

egg also called ba mee or yellow noodles; made from wheat flour and eggs, sold fresh or dried. Range in size from very fine strands to wide, spaghetti-like pieces as thick as a shoelace.

fried crispy egg noodles that have been deep-fried then packaged for sale on supermarket shelves.

hokkien also called stir-fry noodles. These fresh wheat noodles look like thick, yellow-brown spaghetti needing no pre-cooking before use.

rice vermicelli also known as sen mee, mei fun or bee hoon. Used in spring rolls and cold salads; similar to bean threads, only longer and made with rice flour instead of mung bean starch. Before using, soak dried noodles in hot water until softened; boil briefly, rinse with hot water. Vermicelli can also be deep-fried until crunchy and used in salad, as a garnish or as bed for sauces.

soba thin, pale-brown noodle originally from Japan; made from buckwheat and varying proportions of wheat flour. Available dried and fresh, and flavoured (e.g. green tea); eaten in soups, stir-fries, chilled, on their own.

oil

olive made from ripened olives. Extra virgin and virgin are from the first and second press, respectively, and are therefore considered the best; those labelled "extra light" or "light" refer to taste not fat levels.

peanut pressed from ground peanuts; most commonly used oil in Asian cooking because of its capacity to handle high heat without burning.

sesame made from roasted, crushed, white sesame seeds; is used as a flavouring rather than a cooking medium.

vegetable a number of oils sourced from plant rather than animal fats.

onion

green also known as scallion or (incorrectly) shallot; an immature onion picked before the bulb has formed, having a long, bright-green edible stalk.

red also called spanish, red spanish; a sweet-flavoured, large, purple-red onion.

shallots also called french shallots, golden shallots or eschalots. Small, elongated, brown-skinned member of the onion family; they grow in tight clusters similar to garlic.

oyster sauce Asian in origin, this thick, richly flavoured brown sauce is made from oysters and their brine, cooked with salt and soy sauce, and thickened with starches.

pancetta an Italian unsmoked bacon, pork belly cured in salt and spices then rolled into a sausage shape and dried for several weeks. Used, sliced or chopped, as an ingredient rather than eaten on its own

papaya also known as pawpaw.

patty-pan squash also called crookneck or custard marrow pumpkins; a round, slightly flat summer squash being yellow to pale green in colour and having a scalloped edge. Harvested young, it has firm white flesh and a distinct flavour.

prawn also known as shrimp.

preserved lemon preserved in salt, oil or lemon juice, for about

30 days; lemon must be rinsed well before being either chopped.

radicchio Italian in origin; a member of the chicory family. The dark burgundy leaves and strong, bitter flavour can be cooked or eaten raw.

ready-rolled puff pastry packaged sheets of frozen puff pastry, available from supermarkets.

rice

aborio small, round grain rice, well-suited to absorbing a lot of liquid.

basmati a white, fragrant long-grained rice, the grains fluff up when cooked; wash several times before cooking.

jasmine or Thai jasmine, is a long-grained white rice with a perfumed aromatic quality; moist in texture, it clings together after cooking.

rice paper sheets also called banh trang is made from rice flour and water then stamped into rounds. Are quite brittle and break easily; dip briefly in water to make them pliable.

rocket also known as arugula, rugula and rucola; peppery green leaf eaten raw in salads or used in cooking. Baby rocket leaves are smaller and less peppery.

sambal oelek also ulek or olek; Indonesian in origin, this is a salty paste made from ground chillies and vinegar.

sherry fortified wine; they differ in colour and flavour; sold as fino (light, dry), amontillado (medium sweet, dark) and oloroso (full-bodied, very dark).

sichuan peppercorns also known as szechuan or Chinese pepper; a mildly hot spice. Although not related to the peppercorn family, its small, red-brown aromatic berries do look like black peppercorns and have a distinctive peppery-lemon flavour and aroma.

soy sauce also called sieu; made from fermented soybeans. Several varieties are available in supermarkets and Asian food stores; we use Japanese soy sauce unless stated otherwise.

dark deep brown, almost black in colour; rich, with a thicker consistency than other types. Pungent but not particularly salty, it is good for marinating.

japanese all-purpose low-sodium soy sauce with more wheat content than Chinese soy sauces; fermented in barrels and aged. The best table soy and the one to choose if you only want one variety.

light fairly thin in consistency and, while paler than the others, is the saltiest tasting; used in dishes when the natural colour of the ingredients is to

be maintained. Not to be confused with salt-reduced or low-sodium soy sauces.

spinach also known as english spinach and, incorrectly, silverbeet. Baby spinach leaves are eaten raw in salads; larger leaves can be cooked until just wilted.

star anise a dried star-shaped pod; its seeds have an astringent aniseed flavour.

sugar

brown extremely soft, fine granulated sugar retaining molasses for its characteristic colour and flavour.

caster superfine or finely granulated table sugar; dissolves easily.

palm also called nam tan pip, jaggery, jawa or gula melaka; made from the sap of the sugar palm tree. Light brown to black in colour and usually sold in rock-hard cakes; use brown sugar if unavailable.

white coarse, granulated table sugar, also called crystal sugar.

tahini sesame seed paste found in Middle Eastern food stores.

tamari similar to but thicker than japanese soy; very dark in colour with a distinctively mellow flavour.

tamarind the tamarind tree produces clusters of hairy brown pods, each of which is filled with seeds and a viscous pulp, that are dried and pressed into the blocks of tamarind found in Asian food shops. Has a sweet-sour, slightly astringent taste.

concentrate the commercial result of the distillation of tamarind juice into a condensed, compacted paste.

thai basil also called horapa; different from holy basil and sweet basil in look and taste, having smaller leaves and purplish stems, and a slight aniseed taste.

tomato

canned peeled tomatoes in natural juices; available whole, crushed, chopped or diced. Use undrained.

cherry also called tiny tim or tom thumb; small and round.

egg also called plum or roma; smallish, oval-shaped tomatoes used in Italian cooking or salads

paste triple-concentrated puree used to flavour soups, stews and sauces.

semi-dried partially dried tomato pieces in olive oil; softer and juicier than sun-dried, these are not a preserve thus do not keep as long as sun-dried.

sun-dried tomato pieces that have been dried with salt; this dehydrates the tomato and concentrates the flavour. We use sun-dried tomatoes packaged in oil, unless otherwise specified.

truss small vine-ripened tomatoes with vine still attached.

turkish bread also called pide. Sold in long (about 45cm) flat loaves as well as individual rounds; made from wheat flour and sprinkled with black onion seeds.

turmeric also known as kamin; is a rhizome related to galangal and ginger. Must be grated or pounded to release its acrid aroma and pungent flavour. Known for the golden colour it imparts, fresh turmeric can be substituted with the more common dried powder.

vine leaves leaves cryovac-packages containing about 60 leaves in brine can be found in Middle Eastern food shops and some delicatessens; these must be well rinsed and dried before using.

vinegar

apple cider made from fermented apples.

balsamic originally from Modena, Italy, there are now many balsamic vinegars on the market ranging in pungency and quality depending on how, and for how long, they have been aged. Quality can be determined up to a point by price; use the most expensive sparingly.

malt made from fermented malt and beech shavings.

raspberry made from fresh raspberries steeped in white wine vinegar.

rice colourless vinegar made from fermented rice and flavoured with sugar and salt. Also known as seasoned rice vinegar; sherry can be substituted.

wasabi an Asian horseradish used to make the pungent, green-coloured sauce traditionally served with Japanese raw fish dishes; sold in powdered or paste form.

watercress one of the cress family, a large group of peppery greens. Highly perishable, it must be used as soon as possible after purchase.

wombok also called chinese cabbage, peking or napa cabbage; elongated in shape with pale green, crinkly leaves.

wonton wrappers and gow gee or spring roll pastry sheets, made of flour, egg and water, are found in the refrigerated or freezer section of Asian food shops and many supermarkets. These come in different thicknesses and shapes. Thin wrappers work best in soups, while the thicker ones are best for frying; and the choice of round or square, small or large is dependent on the recipe.

zucchini also known as courgette.

index

conversion chart

MEASURES

One Australian metric measuring cup holds approximately 250ml, one Australian metric tablespoon holds 20ml, one Australian metric teaspoon holds 5ml.

The difference between one country's measuring cups and another's is within a two- or three-teaspoon variance, and will not affect your cooking results.North America, New Zealand and the United Kingdom use a 15ml tablespoon.

All cup and spoon measurements are level. The most accurate way of measuring dry ingredients is to weigh them. When measuring liquids, use a clear glass or plastic jug with the metric markings.

We use large eggs with an average weight of 60g.

LIQUID MEASURES

METRIC	IMPERIAL
30ml	1 fluid oz
60ml	2 fluid oz
100ml	3 fluid oz
125ml	4 fluid oz
150ml	5 fluid oz (¼ pint/1 gill)
190ml	6 fluid oz
250ml	8 fluid oz
300ml	10 fluid oz (½ pint)
500ml	16 fluid oz
600ml	20 fluid oz (1 pint)
1000ml (1 litre)	1¾ pints

LENGTH MEASURES

METRIC	IMPERIAL
3mm	⅛in
6mm	¼in
1cm	½in
2cm	¾in
2.5cm	1in
5cm	2in
6cm	2½in
8cm	3in
10cm	4in
13cm	5in
15cm	6in
18cm	7in
20cm	8in
23cm	9in
25cm	10in
28cm	11in
30cm	12in (1ft)

DRY MEASURES

METRIC	IMPERIAL
15g	½oz
30g	1oz
60g	2oz
90g	3oz
125g	4oz (¼lb)
155g	5oz
185g	6oz
220g	7oz
250g	8oz (½lb)
280g	9oz
315g	10oz
345g	11oz
375g	12oz (¾lb)
410g	13oz
440g	14oz
470g	15oz
500g	16oz (1lb)
750g	24oz (1½lb)
1kg	32oz (2lb)

OVEN TEMPERATURES

These oven temperatures are only a guide for conventional ovens.
For fan-forced ovens, check the manufacturer's manual.

	°C (CELSIUS)	°F (FAHRENHEIT)	GAS MARK
Very slow	120	250	½
Slow	150	275 – 300	1 – 2
Moderately slow	160	325	3
Moderate	180	350 – 375	4 – 5
Moderately hot	200	400	6
Hot	220	425 – 450	7 – 8
Very hot	240	475	9

Editorial director Susan Tomnay
Creative director Hieu Chi Nguyen
Food director Pamela Clark
Food editor Louise Patniotis
Senior editor Stephanie Kistner
Designer Caryl Wiggins
Nutrition information Belinda Farlow
Director of sales Brian Cearnes
Marketing manager Bridget Cody
Business analyst Ashley Davies

Chief executive officer Ian Law
Group publisher Pat Ingram
General manager Christine Whiston
Editorial director (WW) Deborah Thomas

WW food team Lyndey Milan, Alexandra Elliott, Frances Abdallaoui

Produced by ACP Books, Sydney.
Printing by Toppan Printing Co., China.
Published by ACP Books, a division of ACP Magazines Ltd,
54 Park St, Sydney; GPO Box 4088, Sydney, NSW 2001
phone +61 2 9282 8618 fax +61 2 9267 9438
acpbooks@acpmagazines.com.au www.acpbooks.com.au
To order books phone 136 116 (within Australia)
Send recipe enquiries to recipeenquiries@acpmagazines.com.au

RIGHTS ENQUIRIES
Laura Bamford, Director ACP Books
lbamford@acpuk.com

Australia Distributed by Network Services,
phone +61 2 9282 8777 fax +61 2 9264 3278
networkweb@networkservicescompany.com.au
United Kingdom Distributed by Australian Consolidated Press (UK),
phone (01604) 642 200 fax (01604) 642 300
books@acpuk.com
New Zealand Distributed by Netlink Distribution Company,
phone (9) 366 9966
ask@ndc.co.nz
South Africa Distributed by PSD Promotions,
phone (27 11) 392 6065/6/7 fax (27 11) 392 6079/80
orders@psdprom.co.za

Clark, Pamela.
Fast seafood
ISBN 978-1-86396-651-1
1. Cookery (Seafood).
I. Title. II. Title: Australian women's weekly.
641.692
© ACP Magazines Ltd 2007
ABN 18 053 273 546
This publication is copyright. No part of it may be reproduced or transmitted in any
form without the written permission of the publishers.

Cover Mustard-seed chilli prawns, page 271
Photographer Louise Lister
Stylist Stephanie Souvlis
Food preparation Ariarne Bradshaw
Acknowledgments to The Sydney Fish Markets.